AF806381

Research Series on the Chinese Dream and China's Development Path

Project Director

Xie Shouguang, President, Social Sciences Academic Press

Series Editors

Li Yang, Chinese Academy of Social Sciences, Beijing, China
Li Peilin, Chinese Academy of Social Sciences, Beijing, China

Academic Advisors

Cai Fang, Gao Peiyong, Li Lin, Li Qiang, Ma Huaide, Pan Jiahua, Pei Changhong, Qi Ye, Wang Lei, Wang Ming, Zhang Yuyan, Zheng Yongnian, Zhou Hong

Drawing on a large body of empirical studies done over the last two decades, this Series provides its readers with in-depth analyses of the past and present and forecasts for the future course of China's development. It contains the latest research results made by members of the Chinese Academy of Social Sciences. This series is an invaluable companion to every researcher who is trying to gain a deeper understanding of the development model, path and experience unique to China. Thanks to the adoption of Socialism with Chinese characteristics, and the implementation of comprehensive reform and opening-up, China has made tremendous achievements in areas such as political reform, economic development, and social construction, and is making great strides towards the realization of the Chinese dream of national rejuvenation. In addition to presenting a detailed account of many of these achievements, the authors also discuss what lessons other countries can learn from China's experience.

More information about this series at http://www.springer.com/series/13571

Peng Zhou

The Theory and Practice of China's Tourism Economy (1978–2017)

SSAP

Springer

Peng Zhou
College of Economics and Management
Zhejiang Normal University
Jinhua, Zhejiang, China

Translated by Shen Jicheng

First published in China by Zhejiang People's Publishing House in 2018.

ISSN 2363-6866 ISSN 2363-6874 (electronic)
Research Series on the Chinese Dream and China's Development Path
ISBN 978-981-32-9106-5 ISBN 978-981-32-9107-2 (eBook)
https://doi.org/10.1007/978-981-32-9107-2

Jointly published with Social Sciences Academic Press, Beijing, China
The print edition is not for sale in China Mainland. Customers from China Mainland please order the print book from: Social Sciences Academic Press, Beijing, China.

© Social Sciences Academic Press and Springer Nature Singapore Pte Ltd. 2019
This work is subject to copyright. All rights are reserved by the Publishers, whether the whole or part of the material is concerned, specifically the rights of translation, reprinting, reuse of illustrations, recitation, broadcasting, reproduction on microfilms or in any other physical way, and transmission or information storage and retrieval, electronic adaptation, computer software, or by similar or dissimilar methodology now known or hereafter developed.
The use of general descriptive names, registered names, trademarks, service marks, etc. in this publication does not imply, even in the absence of a specific statement, that such names are exempt from the relevant protective laws and regulations and therefore free for general use.
The publishers, the authors, and the editors are safe to assume that the advice and information in this book are believed to be true and accurate at the date of publication. Neither the publishers nor the authors or the editors give a warranty, express or implied, with respect to the material contained herein or for any errors or omissions that may have been made. The publishers remain neutral with regard to jurisdictional claims in published maps and institutional affiliations.

This Springer imprint is published by the registered company Springer Nature Singapore Pte Ltd.
The registered company address is: 152 Beach Road, #21-01/04 Gateway East, Singapore 189721, Singapore

Series Preface

Since China's reform and opening began in 1978, the country has come a long way on the path of Socialism with Chinese Characteristics, under the leadership of the Communist Party of China. Over 30 years of reform efforts and sustained spectacular economic growth have turned China into the world's second largest economy, and wrought many profound changes in the Chinese society. These historically significant developments have been garnering increasing attention from scholars, governments, and the general public alike around the world since the 1990s, when the newest wave of China studies began to gather steam. Some of the hottest topics have included the so-called "China miracle", "Chinese phenomenon", "Chinese experience", "Chinese path", and the "Chinese model". Homegrown researchers have soon followed suit. Already hugely productive, this vibrant field is putting out a large number of books each year, with Social Sciences Academic Press alone having published hundreds of titles on a wide range of subjects.

Because most of these books have been written and published in Chinese, however, readership has been limited outside China—even among many who study China—for whom English is still the lingua franca. This language barrier has been an impediment to efforts by academia, business communities, and policy-makers in other countries to form a thorough understanding of contemporary China, of what is distinct about China's past and present may mean not only for her future but also for the future of the world. The need to remove such an impediment is both real and urgent, and the *Research Series on the Chinese Dream and China's Development Path* is my answer to the call.

This series features some of the most notable achievements from the last 20 years by scholars in China in a variety of research topics related to reform and opening. They include both theoretical explorations and empirical studies, and cover economy, society, politics, law, culture, and ecology, the six areas in which reform and opening policies have had the deepest impact and farthest-reaching consequences for the country. Authors for the series have also tried to articulate their visions of the "Chinese Dream" and how the country can realize it in these fields and beyond.

All of the editors and authors for the *Research Series on the Chinese Dream and China's Development Path* are both longtime students of reform and opening and recognized authorities in their respective academic fields. Their credentials and expertise lend credibility to these books, each of which having been subject to a rigorous peer review process for inclusion in the series. As part of the Reform and Development Program under the State Administration of Press, Publication, Radio, Film and Television of the People's Republic of China, the series is published by Springer, a Germany-based academic publisher of international repute, and distributed overseas. I am confident that it will help fill a lacuna in studies of China in the era of reform and opening.

Xie Shouguang

Introduction

The tourism industry is composed of three major parts, namely, tourism resources, tourism facilities, and tourism services. Based on tourism resources and tourism facilities, tourism is actually a comprehensive industry which is particularly or mainly engaged in providing a package of services to tourists, including transportation, accommodation, sightseeing, catering, shopping, entertainment and so on. Tourism, as a human activity, emerged long ago, but as an industrial activity, it came merely a bit after China's reform and opening up starting in 1978.

Before the reform and opening up, tourism in China was solely regarded as part of the country's foreign affairs. Though tourism then played a positive role in promoting friendship and exchanges with the outside world, it did not yet have the characteristics of a modern industry. Since the reform and opening up, China's tourism industry has witnessed a tremendous growth and has become an important drive for its social and economic development. After 40 years' of rapid development since 1978, China's tourism reception scale and international competitiveness have witnessed huge improvement within the period, and its impact on the global tourism has become prominent day by day. Being the world largest tourist exporting country, and with increased comprehensive competitiveness in the global tourism market, China now is playing a more and more important role in the international tourism arena, which further enhances its contribution to the global tourism economy.

The changes of China's tourism industry can be summarized as follows: first, the domestic tourism market has transformed from the niche market to the public one, endowing China with the largest domestic tourism consumption market in the world. With the growth in economy and national income, the per-capita travel had jumped from 0.2 in 1984 to 3 in 2015, increased by 14 times; the number of domestic tourists had expanded from 200 million in 1984 to 40,00 million in 2015, with an increase of 19 times; an average annual growth of 10.2% had been achieved over those years. Secondly, China's international tourism has changed from single inbound tourism to a balanced growth between inbound and outbound tourism. China's outbound tourism market has huge potential for development, and its tourists have become an important force to stimulate the growth of world tourism industry. The country's foreign exchange income of tourism had increased from 263 million US dollars in 1978 to 113.5 billion US dollars in 2015, up by 431 times and an annual average increase of 17.8%.

Thirdly, the role of tourism in China has transformed from pure foreign affairs reception in the beginning to the current mutual development between its past role and the role of being an industry, and the integrated function of China's tourism is becoming increasingly prominent. China's tourism is switching from a general industry to a strategic pillar industry, with both its industry scale and capacity growing rapidly. The tapping of tourism industry has extended from parts of the country to the whole, thus forging a big industry pushed forward both by the local and central governments, governments and enterprises, as well as the society as a whole.

In the beginning of China's reform and opening up, the development of tourism industry in China was seen merely in several hot tourist cities, such as Beijing, Shanghai, Xi'an, and Guilin together with a few famous scenic spots, such as Mount Huangshan, Mount Emei, etc. Whereas, China's tourism development has now expanded to the whole country and the whole world, being an important driving force for local and national economic growth. And it is still moving forward rapidly, with the building of world first-class tourist destination, cities, counties and provinces as its main aims, and the development of tourism enterprises, brands, products, colleges, as well as the cultivation of tourist talents as its major goals.

Great achievements have been made with China's tourism within such a short period of time, so many of its management concepts, methods, and service capabilities though started from scratch, having become diverse and more mature. Therefore, the experience, concepts and wisdom with Chinese characteristics shown in its tourism development are increasingly attracting the attention of the whole world.

The year 2018 marks the 40th anniversary of China's reform and opening-up[1]. This book aims to review the achievements made in theory and practice of China's development of its tourism economy over the past 40 years. In the process of writing this book, the author has referred to the relevant tourism Yearbooks, government work reports, academic papers, periodicals and works, and reviewed and quoted the research results of a large number of domestic scholars and various research reports. Moreover, some of my postgraduates of different grades contributed more or less to the book in collecting data and materials. The author would

[1]The 40 years of reform and opening up referred to in this paper is generally regarded as the period from 1978 to 2018. Anyhow, the data in this paper are only updated to 2017, currently the latest data available in the national statistical yearbooks which can be collected by far, while the data of 2018 are not released yet.

like to express his sincere gratitude to them all here. The author would also be grateful to any criticisms of the book, so that further improvement and correction can be made on the book in the future.

August 2018 Zhou Peng

Contents

Chapter 1
General Introduction to Industrialized Development of Tourism Since China's Reform and Opening-Up

Since the beginning of China's reform and opening-up that started in 1978, Chinese people's knowledge on tourism industry has been gradually reaching profundity. In the period of the reform, the tourism industry had been rapidly developed. Its nature had been transformed from a business structure into an industry. Its market had become stronger in an open environment and its system had been changed from a single system into a comprehensive one. Its tourism products have been diversified contrary to the simple sightseeing that existed in the beginning. In this chapter a relatively systematical analysis and summary of China's tourism development will be made based on a large number of relevant materials.

1.1 Summary of Industrialized Tourism Development Process Since China's Reform and Opening-Up

1.1.1 Development of Tourism Industry: Rapid Positioning in the Reform

Since 1978, China had experienced a gradual deepening process on the understanding of the tourism industry. Being a diplomatic business in the beginning, it was transformed into an economic industry and later transformed into a comprehensive industry. Its nature had been equally changed step by step alongside its functions which had become richer. And policies related to the tourism industry had become more and more specific. As early as 1978, Deng Xiaoping[1] proposed that ten billion U.S. dollars of foreign exchange earnings should to be collected from tourism; in the following year he also pointed out that tourism should become a comprehensive

[1]Deng Xiaoping (Aug. 1904–Feb. 19), the leader of China from 1978 until his retirement in 1992, renown as the chief architect of China's reform and opening-up since late 1978.

© Social Sciences Academic Press and Springer Nature Singapore Pte Ltd. 2019

P. Zhou, *The Theory and Practice of China's Tourism Economy (1978–2017)*,
Research Series on the Chinese Dream and China's Development Path,
https://doi.org/10.1007/978-981-32-9107-2_1

industry. The core of Deng Xiaoping's thought about the tourism economy is that tourism should be considered as an economic industry (Fig. 1.1).

In 1981, the State Council for the first time, organized and held a National Working Conference on tourism. During this conference, it was clearly stated that the tourism industry was a comprehensive economic business. It was equally stated that the tourism industry is an important element of the national economy and is also an essential business related to national economy and the people's livelihood in general. In 1998, during the Central Economic Working Conference, tourism was defined as a new growth point of national economy. In 2001, in the "Notice for Further Accelerating Tourism" issued by the state council of China, it was strongly proposed that the concept of a big tourism should be built. Such a proposal would certainly fully mobilize the enthusiasm of people in every walk of life, and consequently would give people the possibility to play a role in the tourism sector which was also considered as the new growth point to the national economy. In 2006, it was clearly put forward that tourism would be developed into an important industry of the national economy in the 11th Five-Year Plan outline for China's tourism development. With the continuous rise of the status of tourism by the central government, the provincial governments nationwide have presently released over 60 comments or decisions on tourism development starting with the "Decision on Tourism Development with Great Efforts" released by the Shaanxi Province in 1985. Tourism was defined by 27 provinces as the pillar industry, a leading industry or an important industry. In the 1990s, the state proposed that tourism should be developed as the new economic growth point. The tourism industry has become an important means to expand domes-

Fig. 1.1 Picture of Deng Xiaoping

tic demands. Since the entry into the new century, the international economic environment and the domestic development environment have been greatly changed. The central government considered tourism as an important industry that would increase consumption and that would contribute to the building of an international economic image. Since the holding of the 17th CPC National Congress[2] in 2007, the strategic measures on the development and comprehensive construction of a well-off society have been implemented. More emphasis has been laid on the people's livelihood and the construction of ecological civilization. Tourism has been positioned as an important industry to the national economy and also a comprehensive industry that involves politics, culture, society and ecology etc.

1.1.2 Tourism Market Development: Growing into a Stage of Maturity in an Open Environment

Since the reform and opening-up in late 1978, in order to catch up with the pace of world tourism powers, China's tourism industry has taken a development path which is totally different from the path that was taken by the developed countries in the west. The Western countries generally took national tourism (including domestic tourism and outbound tourism) as the starting point for tourism development; China, when taking into the consideration of its specific national conditions, had followed such a path: from the development of inbound tourism to domestic tourism and then to outbound tourism. The take-off of China's tourism is marked by the exploitation of international tourism market, resulting from its own rich and profound tourism resources, the good external environment brought about by China's reform and opening-up and the various increasingly-improved basic conditions.

In 1978, China received only 720,000 overnight tourist arrivals and which brought in a foreign exchange earnings of 260 million US dollars. By 1987, the number of overnight visitors to China exceeded 10 million. The increase from 40 million tourists to 50 million tourists was achieved within only 3 years. It took China less time for every \$5 billion of increase in tourism foreign exchange to reach \$419.19 billion in 2007, an increase of \$8 billion in just one year compared with 2006. Moreover, China's tourism industry had also witnessed a continuous rise in the world rankings. In 1978, the number of China's international tourist arrivals and the ranking of international tourism income were both below Top 40 in the world. While in 1980, the number of China's international tourists began to enter Top 20, then within Top 10 in 1988, and within Top 5 since 1999. Concerning the ranking of the international tourism receipts, China ranked only 34 globally in 1980. It entered Top 30 in 1982, Top 20 in 1992, Top 10 in 1994 and Top 5 in 2007. It took less than a quarter of a century for China's tourism industry to catch up with and surpass the development pace of tourism in many countries. This had greatly exceeded the original expecta-

[2] 17th CPC National Congress, is the national congress of the Chinese Communist Party which was held in 2007.

tions of scholars from tourism circles at home and abroad and it has also set up a role model for the other developing countries to implement their catch-up strategy.

In the early stage of reform and opening up, China's tourism market was single and weak, focusing mainly on the reception of overseas inbound tourists. Whereas, its domestic tourism was limited to small-scale business trips and certain official activities, not to mention its outbound tourism in a strict sense. After 40 years of development, China is now a major tourism destination country in the world and has witnessed a huge increase in its inbound tourism market. Having gone through rapid rise and accelerated development in the mid-1980s, China's tourist density has reached more than once per capita since 2006, demonstrating the continuous expansion of China's tourism market coverage and the deepening of its market development. With the deepening of opening-up to the outside world, China's outbound tourism has been booming since the mid-late 1990s and China has become an important tourist exporting country in the world. After 40 years of development, China's tourist source market has truly grown into a three-pillar pattern: with the development of outbound travel, inbound travel and domestic travel well balanced.

At the beginning of reform and opening up, under the extremely limited reception facilities and traffic conditions, with rich tourism resources and mysterious Oriental culture as the attraction and the earning of foreign exchange as the goal, the inbound tourism was blooming alone. Regardless of fluctuations, the inbound tourism maintained a high-speed overall growth, like a shining star in the reform and opening-up of that period. In the past 40 years, the number of China's inbound tourists has grown from 1.8092 to 131.8733 million, an annual average growth rate of 15.9%. The number of overnight tourists increased from 720,000 peoples to 54.7198 million, an annual average growth of 16.1%. The international tourism receipts increased from 263 million US dollars to 41.919 billion US dollars, an annual average growth of 19.1 and 10% higher than the similar global tourism index in the same period.

In the early stage of reform and opening-up, limited by various conditions, the Chinese government adopted the policy of "no promotion, no publicity and no opposition" towards domestic tourism. Entering the mid-1980s, with the improvement of comprehensive national strength and the remarkable increase of residents' income, the domestic tourism market came into being. In 1993, "Opinions on the Positive Development of Domestic Tourism" was issued by the China National Tourism Administration (abbreviated as CNTA). In which, the guidelines of "invigorating the market, strengthening the management and improving the quality" were put forward for the development of domestic tourism. Honestly speaking, in order to overcome the inflation caused by economic overheating in the second half of 1993 and the Asian financial crisis in 1997, it was necessary to vigorously develop domestic tourism to expand domestic demand. Under the combined action of the internal and external factors, the domestic tourism was highly valued. Due to the implementation of the two-day weekend system in 1995, Chinese residents had more leisure time. The "golden week" initiated in 2000 brought about the "blowout" phenomenon in domestic tourism during the holidays. This reflects the unique but strong endogenous demand. This had enabled the inbound tourism to become the two wheels driving the development of China's tourism industry. In particular, the "golden week", which started in 2000, led to the blowout of domestic tourism during holidays, which showed the unique and strong internal consumption demand and together with the inbound tourism became the two wheels driving the development of China's tourism industry.

Since 1993, the CNTA had entrusted the National Bureau of Statistics with the mission to carry a yearly sample investigations and statistics on the domestic travels taken by the urban residents from Mainland China. In the 15 years, from 1993 to 2007, the number of domestic tourists increased from 410 million to 1.61 billion, with an annual average growth rate of 10.3%. The domestic tourism income also rose from 86.4 to 777.1 billion yuan, with an annual average growth rate of 17%.

The outbound travel taken by Chinese citizens was an extension and an upgrade of the travel demand and the inevitable result of the reform and opening-up. In October 1990, Chinese citizens were first allowed to travel to Singapore, Malaysia and Thailand at their own expense. Since 1997, on the basis of the pilot travel to Hong Kong, Macao and some neighboring countries, the outbound tourism business was formally launched for Chinese citizens at their own expenses. Thereafter, the number of outbound tourism destinations was gradually increased. By the end of 2007, apart from the two special administrative regions, Hong Kong and Macao, 132 countries had become the outbound tourism destinations for Chinese citizens. After entry into the new century, the number of Chinese citizens traveling abroad has grown rapidly, reaching 40.954 million in 2007, 3.9 times that of 2000. In the same year, the number of private outbound tourists reached 34.924 million, accounting for 85% of the total number of outbound tourists. China now is not only an important tourism destination in the world, but is also a major tourism-generating income country. Over the past 40 years, China's tourism market has been developing vigorously. It has made the leap from a major tourism resource country to an Asian major tourism country and is striding forward to be a world tourism power.

1.1.3 Industrial System: From Single to Comprehensive

In the beginning of reform and opening-up, China's tourism reception facilities and conditions were extremely insufficient and shabby. At that time, except some old hotels left over before 1949 and guest houses built under the planned economy, there were no modern tourist hotels in the country, with only China International Travel Service (CITS) and China Travel Service (CTS) being able to receive foreign tourists. Tourism management and service awareness was basically blank, and even worse, civil aviation and railway traffic became the bottleneck of tourism development. On the condition of such material shortage and supply shortage, China's tourism industry started from scratch. Its tourism supply capacity increased continuously, industrial scale expanded largely, industrial system improved gradually and industrial openness increased day by day. An important factor for the rapid growth of China's tourism industry is that it always adheres to the market orientation and takes the cultivation of industrial system as the center to constantly expand supply, improve quality and meet the ever-growing and increasingly diversified tourism demand.

At the beginning of tourism development, China's shortage of tourism supply was highly correlated with the backwardness of its national economy, especially the shortage of hotels and transportation. In 1981, the State Council's pointed out in "Decision on Strengthening Tourism Work" that the current tourism reception conditions were poor, and the problems should be resolved step by step. In 1979, the first batch of Sino-foreign joint ventures emerged in China, and of which the first three approved were tourism joint ventures, so much so that tourism stood at the forefront of China's opening-up to the outside world. From the early 1970s to the late 1980s, the direct foreign investment in tourism industry used by China was about 5 billion US dollars in total. By introducing huge amounts of foreign investment, the hot tourism cities and economically-developed regions throughout the country set up a batch of new tourist hotels. This gradually relieved the bottleneck of the insufficient accommodation and reception facilities, hence improving the management and service level of China's tourist hotels and also laid a solid foundation for the long-term development of China's tourism industry.

In the mid-1980s, the focus of tourism work was shifted to the cultivation of industrial systems. In 1985, the State Council approved the National Tourism Administration's report on the reform of the current tourism system, saying that emphasis laid on the international tourism shall to be shifted to the international and domestic tourism; the mere reliance on state investment for the construction of tourism infrastructure shall be shifted to the reliance on invest from state, local governments, departments, the collective and individuals as a whole, and self-dependence should go hand in hand with the use of foreign capital; the major emphasis laid on tourism reception shall be shifted to the equal importance on the development and construction of tourism resources and tourism reception. The enactment of these guidelines actively promoted the gathering of capital from various channels for the tourism industry, marking the entry of China's tourism industry into a new stage of constructing its tourism industry system in an all-round way. After 1998, China began to issue national bonds to solve major problems and issues relating to infrastructure construction. From 2000 to 2004, China allocated totally 6.72 billion yuan of bonds for tourism development, and another 2.1 billion yuan for the construction of red tourism[3] from 2005 to 2007 (Fig. 1.2).

Entering the 21st century, China's modern traffic network was gradually set up, which contributed to the breakthrough of traffic bottleneck of tourism as a whole, and also had a significant impact on tourists' travel mode. Concerning the civil aviation, by 2007, China had 148 navigable airports with scheduled flights and equally 146 cities with regular flights. The total length of railway lines in operation throughout China reached 78,000 km, ranking the third in the world. The total highway mileage throughout the country reached 3.5837 million km and the expressway mileage of China's 11 provinces exceeded 2000 km. In addition to regular scheduled flights and trains, tourist-chartered flights, tourist-dedicated trains and self-drive travel became

[3]Red tourism, is a subset of tourism in China where people visit locations with historical significance to China's liberation cause led by the Communist Party of China to mainly pay homage to the revolutionary martyrs and rekindle their long-lost sense of class struggle and proletarian principles.

Fig. 1.2 Red tourism

a trend. The construction of infrastructures on environment protection, information, and energy, etc., was advanced by leaps and bounds, thus providing a better condition for the development of the tourism industry.

By the end of 2007, 18,943 travel agencies came into existence throughout the country, among which 1797 were international travel agencies. Moreover, 13,583 star-rated hotels; more than 20,000 scenic spots and over 3100 Level A scenic spots (including 928 scenic spots and the Level A scenic spots) were built in China. At the same time, 12 state-level tourist resorts and more than 100 province-level tourist resorts were set up, and 307 excellent tourism cities, 17 outstanding tourism counties and 1098 industrial and agricultural tourism demonstration sites were established. In addition, there emerged 187 national key scenic spots, 303 national natural reserves, 627 national forest parks, 138 national geological parks, and 35 of which were listed in the World Heritage Sites. After over 40 years of cultivation and development, China's tourism industry has witnessed the construction of a multi-dimensional system pattern (Fig. 1.3).

The cultivation of China's tourism system went through a gradual change of process from a planned system to a market system or from a closed system to an opened system. Let's take the travel agency for example: at the beginning stage, the inbound tourism was systematically and monopolistically operated by three state-owned monopoly travel agencies, but it was gradually decentralized to more than 10 travel agencies under the control of the central ministries and more than 30 local travel agencies with independent sales right. The travel agencies went through a process of highly planning to full competition. After some time, the restrictions on ownership

Fig. 1.3 Agricultural tourism demonstration sites

were loosened so as to allow the participation of private capital. After China's entry into the World Trade Organization in 2002, the travel agency industry began to open up to the outside world; this significantly speeded up the internationalization process of China's tourism development. Presently, China's travel agency industry has opened up two markets, namely, the foreign capital market and the private capital market, which has consequently led to market competition. By 2007, there were 16 foreign-owned travel agencies in China, 11 being foreign-controlled travel agencies and 8 being travel agencies with foreign equity participation. Apart from these travel agencies, there were equally some large-scale travel groups from the United States, Japan, Germany, Britain and other professional travel agencies specialized in high-end market.

China's cultivation of its tourism industry system was a gradual process, which had transformed from quantity-oriented to quality-oriented and from extensive management to intensive management. The establishment of the export-oriented economy greatly stimulated the supply of tourism production elements. By the end of the 20th century, the industrial factory system of transportation, sightseeing, accommodation, food and beverage, shopping, and entertainment, etc. was completed. After the entry into the new century, with the rapid expansion of the tourism industry scale, the tourism product chain had been expanded. The industrial chain had been improved and the industrial scope had been widened so as to enable the construction of a relatively complete industrial cluster system and a system of labor division and cooperation. This had paved the way for the development of tourism-related industries. With the establishment of market mechanism, the implementation of modern enterprise system, and the intensification of competition on tourism internationalization, and the management of tourism enterprises is gradually changing from extensive to intensive.

China's tourism standardization had played a vital role in the process of the development of its industry system. In 1987, China promulgated the business norm of "Division and Evaluation of the International Tourism Hotel's Star Rating", marking the beginning of its tourism standardization. The National Tourism Standardization Technology Committee was established in 1995 and the National Tourism Quality Certification Management Committee was established in 2001. Both committees devoted to strengthening the guidance and management of the tourism industry towards tourism standardization and quality certification in China. So far, China has enacted 18 tourism standards, including 11 national standards and 7 industrial standards. Hence, China has become the country that has issued the largest number of tourism standards in the world. Tourism standardization has stimulated the standardization construction of its entire service industry. For example, the concept of star rating introduced by touristic hotels has been successfully extended to other industries, and the star grade representing different level of service has a consensus reached by the whole society.

The cultivation of tourism industry system has gone through such a developmental process: From a single system to diversified one and from a partial system to a complete one. As far as touristic product is concerned, the initial product was characterized by single-team sightseeing with a full package price. However, with the development of the society and the economy, and with the continuous improvement of the tourism destination's reception facilities and the exertion of the tourism industry's advantages, great changes have taken place in the variety of tourism products. For instance, the self-drive tourism, official business, exhibition award, leisure vacation, specific tourism and other types of tourism have occupied a larger proportion than before. With regards to tourist destination, China's tourism industry was characterized by sightseeing at the initial development stage, centering mainly on Beijing, Shanghai, Guangzhou, Xi'an, Guilin and a few other hot tourism cities. With the diversification of the tourism market, tourism in central cities of all levels and types keeps emerging, which drives the development of tourism in surrounding areas and forms a block dominated by regional tourism. As far as the industrial form is concerned, a group of touristic attractions, tourism facilities and tourism enterprises have emerged. The following are some typical examples: the top attractions represented by more than 30 world cultural and natural heritages; the outstanding tourist spots represented by Mount Huangshan (in Central China), Jiuzhaigou Valley (in West

China) and Overseas Chinese Town[4] (in South China) etc.; the city-type tourism destinations represented by Chengdu, Dalian, Hangzhou, Sanya, etc.; the high-end touristic hotels represented by Platinum 5-Star Hotel and the economy hotels represented by Home Inn and Jinjiang Inn; the inland river Sightseeing cruises represented by the Yangtze River cruise; the comprehensive tourism groups represented by China National Travel Service (HK) Group Corporation and Beijing Tourism Group; the professional hotel groups represented by Jinjiang Inn, New Century, etc.; the tourism e-commerce operators represented by Ctrip, Elong, etc.; the tourism recreational projects represented by *Impression Liu Sanjie*, and *Reflection of Yunnan*, etc. On the whole, it has formed a product and service system that can meet the different needs of domestic and foreign tourists and an industrial cluster with destination as the core (Fig. 1.4).

The cultivation of tourism industry system is a process of the development of the tourism market production elements. In the management of the tourism industry, various production elements play a basic and fundamental role. As far as the resource factor is concerned, China is a country rich in tourism resources. However, the problem is how to optimize the allocation of various factors of production, such as land, talent, information and technology, culture, management, capital and prop-

Fig. 1.4 Jiuzhaigou, Sichuan

[4]Overseas Chinese Town, is a scenic spot in Shenzhen City, Guangdong Province, China, near Huaqiaocheng Station on the Shenzhen Metro, classified as an Five A-level scenic area by China National Tourism Administration.

erty rights, and so on. Moreover, in different stages of development, different factors of production have different degrees of restriction, and the restrictions are shifting. In the 1980s, the tourism sector in China was characterized by the abundance in resources but insufficiency in funds. In the beginning, the problem was the shortage of hotels, and later, there came weaknesses in the traffic and various kinds of tourism production materials so that the investment attraction was carried out on a large scale. In the early 1990s, with the gradual growth of the tourism market and the comprehensive development of the production elements, the diversified market subjects constantly emerged, leading to the vigorous development of China's tourism industry. In the process of tourism development, the major contradiction was also shifted from the restriction of the hard elements of production, such as fund, land, etc. to that of the soft elements of production, such as talent, information, technology, brand, management, etc.

The cultivation of tourism industry system is a process of dynamic improvement and continuous innovation. With the increasingly intensified competition in domestic and overseas tourism markets, the innovation awareness of tourism destinations and operators has also been increased. With regards to the constant development of new resources, the constant emergence of new products and the application of new technologies, an extreme challenge has been imposed on the traditional mode of operation, thus increasing the difficulty for enterprises to survive and inspiring the enterprises' eagerness for innovation. In the process of development, the tourism industry has continuously generated new fields and formats, such as leisure vacation, digital tourism, exhibition and incentive tourism, economy hotel, cruise and yacht, live performance, tourism intelligence, etc. With the entry into the new century, new tourism products have been constantly developed, such as ecological tourism, rural tourism, industrial tourism, red tourism, military tourism, hot-spring tourism, ice-snow tourism, health tourism, science-technology tourism etc. These new products have effectively propelled changes in product structure, the industrial structure and the market tourism structure. The tourism industry has transformed the traditional industries and improved the traditional businesses. It has also constantly created new fields to constitute a new format. This is the inevitable result of tourism development and innovation, as well as the fundamental way to improve the competitiveness of China's tourism industry. Hence representing the future of the tourism industry and also embodying the new direction of the tourism industry (Fig. 1.5).

1.1.4 Change of Tourism Management Mode: From Micro to Macro

The change in the tourism management mode arose from the understanding of tourism attribute and reform on tourism economic system. The tourism industry has gone through an evolution process of enterprise management, industrial management and public management. The transition started from the foreign reception.

Fig. 1.5 Industrial tourism

In the beginning, China's tourism industry was under the administrative control of the government and the planned economy mode under the direct management of the government was implemented. During that early stage, the main subjects of the tourism management were travel agencies and touristic hotels. In December 1964, upon the basis of the China International Travel Service Head Office, China Travel and Sightseeing Bureau was set up as a department directly under the State Council and in the charge of the Ministry of Foreign Affairs. This bureau was co-located with China International Travel Service Head Office to execute the practice of two organizations but with the same staff. In March 1978, its name was changed to China Administration of Travel and Sightseeing but it still stayed as a department directly under the State Council and under the control of the Ministry of Foreign Affairs. In August 1982, after the approval of the Standing Committee of the National People's Congress, the China Administration of Travel and Sightseeing was changed to China National Tourism Administration (CNTA) of The People's Republic of China. This name lasted for a short period of time. In July 1982, the office of the CNTA and China International Travel Service Head Office was separated, but the former still held the right of outreach notification, the right of travel package price fixing and other management rights involving foreign interests. The rights of outreach and visa notification were not attributed to the province-level institutions till January 1985.

Since China's reform and opening-up, the complicated national conditions, vast territory, low level of economic development, imperfect infrastructure, immature market economy development and other special national conditions of China imposed a necessity to implement the government-leading strategy for tourism development. As the status of the tourism industry was increasingly raised in the national economy, the governments at all levels also gave more support for the development of the industry. In 1985, the State Council approved the *National Tourism Development Planning* (1986–2000) which for the first time, regarded the tourism industry as a state-supported undertaking and it was included in the national economic development plan. In 1986, the State Council set up a tourism coordination group, marking the entry into a new stage of development of China's tourism industry. In the same year, the State Council issued the first tourism administrative regulation, "Interim Regulations on the Management of Travel Agencies". In 1988, the National Tourism Committee was set up, which was a standing deliberation and coordination agency under the State Council and had as mission to further strengthen the guidance of the tourism industry. In the same year, the General Office of the State Council approved by the State Council forwarded "Suggestions Concerning the Strengthening of Tourism Work", which was submitted by the CNTA to clarify the scope of the tourism industry in principle.

In October 1988, the State Council issued the scheme of "three functions" for China National Tourism Administration. This granted the CNTA the functions to: "Draft the facility and service standards for various tourist attractions, resorts and tourist accommodations, travel agencies, tourism automobiles and cruises and specific tourism projects, as well as to organize the corresponding implementations"; to "formulate the occupational qualification standards and grade standards for tourist practitioners; to direct the corresponding implementations". This scheme stated clearly the responsibilities and the functions of the department of tourism and from that time on, the tourism industry gradually turned to the path of economic management. Under the State Council's unified deployment in 1998, the government-enterprise decoupling policy was implemented for China International Travel Service Head Office, Beijing International Hotel and other enterprises directly under the CNTA. In May 1999, the enterprise directly under Beijing Municipal Administration of Tourism was separated from the organization to establish Beijing Tourism Group, thus driving the system changes throughout the country and marking entry of the management system of the tourism enterprise into a new stage.

Alongside the increasingly deepened reform and opening-up, the accelerated transformation of the economic society, the constantly enriched tourism practice and the gradually deepened knowledge on the law of tourism development, in terms of content, scope, methods and means etc., compared with that which existed at the initial stage of reform and opening-up, the tourism management mode had been greatly changed. In 1999, after the CNTA had put forward the target to build China into a world tourism power, the focus of the tourism industry management was shifted from travel agency and hotel industry to macro tourism, macro market and macro industry; meanwhile, a series of industrial management regulations and measures were issued in succession to promote the development in depth and breadth of tourism management. In 2000, the State Council promulgated "Regulation on Public Holidays for National Annual Festivals and Memorial Day and the Opinions on Further Developing the Holiday Tourism". The state council also set up the national holiday tourism inter-ministerial coordination meeting system to vigorously develop the holiday tourism economy.

Industry associations are an important part of the tourism management system. Upon the approval of the State Council, the first tourism industry organization, China Tourism Association, was officially established in January 1986. After more than 20 years of development, the professional fields of the tourism industry association has been constantly enriched and the number of members has also continuously increased. In the regional structure, 31 provinces, municipalities and autonomous regions throughout the country have established tourism associations. In terms of industry structure, various professional tourism associations organized according to the tourism elements have been distributed in various regions at different levels. Covering the major enterprises and institutions of the six tourism elements, namely "food and beverage, accommodation, transportation, sightseeing, shopping and entertainment", the members of the tourism industry association included touristic cities, tourism enterprise groups, travel agencies, star-rated hotels, scenic spots, tourism research institutes, and tourism media, etc.; meanwhile, the asset scale and market share of the members occupied a decisive position in national tourism so much so that they have become the backbone force that promotes the development of China's tourism industry. With the continuous growth of market economy, being the link between the government and market subjects, the tourism industry association is increasingly playing an important role and has gradually become the implementation subject for industry service, coordination, supervision and self-regulation.

Over the past 40 years (from 1978 to 2008), the tourism management system has been changed, resulting in the functional transformation of government regulation, domination and guidance to service and supervision. The management object was shifted from the management of the subordinate enterprise to the management of the travel agency and hotel industry and was also extended to the management of the whole tourism industry. The development of touristic attractions was shifted to the construction of tourism destinations, while the single department and single industry were expanded into an entire industry, destination and society. The management tool was shifted from the single administrative instruction to guiding and directing of the enterprises through the formulation of national and industrial standards etc. The management scope was expanded from the regulation of the tourism practitioners to focusing and satisfying the tourism demands of the residents and the masses. More so, the management concept was shifted from the pursuit of economic profit to the focus on social economy, cultural education, environmental protection, protection of heritage, human values, national image and other comprehensive benefits. Presently, according to the scientific concept of "people-orientation", the tourism management is undergoing a further change. According to the requirements to construct a "service-oriented government", the tourism management departments at all levels are sparing no effort to realize functional transformation, strengthen the construction of public service, promote the tourism development achievements to benefit the masses and accelerate the construction of a service guarantee system oriented towards the domestic and the overseas tourists.

The process of development, reform and innovation of China's tourism management system and the achievements has proven that the institutional arrangement and innovation and government's leading role are the key factors to promote a healthy and fast development of the tourism industry in a country or region. After years of efforts, China's tourism management system has basically transformed into a mode adapting to China's national conditions, and major institutional obstacles to the development of tourism have been basically eliminated. In the meantime, it has been initially proposed that the government-leading tourism development strategy be implemented under the market economy, which will in turn lay a solid foundation for realizing the goal of constructing China into a tourism power.

1.1.5 Tourism Market Development: From Publicizing to Marketing

In the initial stage of the tourism, due to the restrictions caused by the shortage of supply, the main goal of tourism was the management of supply. Owing to the gradually increased tourism service facilities and the increasingly intensified competition in the tourism market, the main objective of tourism has been shifted to supply and demand management. Oriented towards demand, the tourism industry attached great importance to marketing, which is also a common practice undertaken by the tourism industry of various countries in the world and reflects the requirement of internal law of tourism development.

Before and at the beginning of the reform and opening-up, there was no such thing as marketing tourism in China. In the early 1980s, China's tourism publicity achieved some progress. From 1981, China started to successively set up travel agencies in Tokyo, Paris, New York, London, Frankfurt, Sydney, Los Angeles and other cities. The CNTA set up a publicity department in 1983, and established an international market development department in 1988 respectively. Both departments were in charge of studying and formulating strategies to develop the international market and formulate concrete measures; to perform external publicity and to develop international tourist source market. By the end of 1980s, China had initially established an institutional system of tourism market promotion from the central government to local governments, from tourism management departments to various tourism enterprises.

Before the 1990s, China's tourism was based on the single inbound tourism demand, and China's tourism publicity was merely focusing on the overseas market. In the early 1990s, with the vigorous development of domestic tourism, the proportion of funds invested by the state and local governments in the promotion of domestic tourism market also became larger and larger. In 1991, the top 40 tourist attractions in China were selected. Tough the selection campaign was still oriented at inbound tourists, yet with the rapid rise of the domestic tourism market, it had promoted both internal and external markets. Since the mid-1990s, tourism has been taken as the pillar industry or key industry in various regions, and the investment in domestic market promotion has been increasingly strengthened. In 1998, the central government clearly defined the tourism industry as a new growth point of the national economy and the focus of the tourism marketing had also led to its fundamental transformation, that is, the focus on international market was shifted to the domestic and international markets.

Over the past 40 years, the focus of the tourism marketing has shown a trend of gradually moving downwards while the means and the degree of specialization of tourism promotion have been constantly improved. After the entry into the 1990s, provinces, municipalities and autonomous regions started to carry out the diversified marketing strategies, touristic cities in particular had increasingly become subjects in tourism market promotion. In the meantime, the choice of tourism media also became more diverse. The tourism media evolved from magazine, brochure and other written materials to TV, Internet, VCD, elaborate tourism atlas, distinctive local tourist guide book, mobile phone text message, etc. Thus, the single means of marketing was replaced by the complex, large-scale, multi-angle, all-round and internationally-compatible marketing mode. In 1997, the CNTA officially launched the first national website for China's tourism, in which the government departments took the lead in entering into the era of "information superhighway". In January 2002, the first domestic professional tourism satellite television channel, namely Tourism General Channel (Tourism Satellite TV) (abbreviated TSTV) of Hainan Television Station, was formally launched, thus pioneering the professional tourism television media. In October 2002, the first tourism destination marketing system (DMS) of China, namely Guangdong Nanhai DMS, was officially completed, symbolizing the informatization construction of China's tourism promotion. Initiated in 1998, China International Travel Mart (CITM) had been successfully held for 13 consecutive terms by the year 2011, and it had become an annual international tourism festival in Asia featured by large scale and highest degree of specialization and internationalization.

1.1.6 International Development: From Introducing to Blending

China's tourism is blended with the world tourism, constituting a relatively complete internationalization process of China's tourism industry. It is mainly embodied in five aspects: Firstly, China had joined the world tourism organization and the various international organizations; Secondly, the entry of foreign-funded hotel groups and management companies; Thirdly, the entry of foreign-funded travel agencies; Fourthly, the foreign capital is fully involved in the tourism industry; Fifthly, the "going-out" process of China's tourism industry. Originating from inbound tourism, the tourism industry is the pioneer promoter of China's opening-up to the outside world. Taking advantage of the international capital, experience and technology has always been a shortcut to improve the development of the tourism industry. According to the relevant statistical data of the Ministry of Commerce, by the end of 2006, in the field of China's tourism services, there had been 3347 projects in total using the foreign direct investment: the accumulative contract amount of foreign capital had reached 12.721 billion US dollars while the accumulative amount of the actual use of foreign capital had risen to 7.279 billion US dollars. In addition to the use of foreign capital, measures like learning from international experience, attracting international talents, introducing international planning, conducting international bidding, etc. have also been adopted. The taking of these actions, on the one hand, had narrowed the gap existing in tourism development between China and the West; on the other hand, the core competitiveness China's tourism had been developed.

China's tourism industry adheres to policy of the reform and opening-up to the overseas market and the non-loosening to the domestic market. The opening-up to the overseas market constituted the internationalization process of China's tourism while the unloosening to the domestic market has constituted the marketization process of China's tourism. At the early stage, China's opening-up focused on attracting foreign capital and foreigners. With the acceleration of economic development, the focus of the later liberalization was mainly on the domestic citizens and enterprises, with an eye to the establishment of a unified national market. After China's accession into the World Trade Organization (WTO) in 2001, the opening-up of its tourism industry to both internal and external markets was gradually coordinated. The national treatment was implemented both to the domestic and foreign capital. Moreover, apart from some fields, the restrictive measures on the tourism industry in the aspect of market access had been basically lifted. In the process of opening-up, the entry of the foreign capital and the development of private enterprises constituted the two dominant factors in the tourism industry. Although the entry of foreign capital was not in large scale, it played a key role in the key segments, thus producing a profound social influence. In the meantime, though the development of private tourism capital did not start earlier enough, due to rapid development, it had created a batch of enterprises (groups) characterized for sound management structure and powerful economic strength, therefore constituted an important driving force to promote the development of tourism.

With the entry into the new century, China's tourism industry presents a new trend of nationalization of international competition and internationalization of domestic market. Nearly all the world's largest hotel companies and tourism groups have entered China, thus enabling the international competition to be unfolded on the Chinese territory. After internationalization, the domestic market of China had become a strategic point for multinational companies. The internationalization of domestic market shows that the tourism companies of China not only have to compete with the local operators, but also have to compete with the multinational companies which had been established in China in order to contend for the Chinese market. This is known as the globalization process of China's tourism industry.

Based on the catch-up development path, China's tourism industry has been emphasizing the integration with international standards for many years. After China's accession to the WTO, under the encouragement of national policy, the "going out" pace of China's tourism enterprises and operators has obviously been accelerated; meanwhile, with the rapid development of China's outbound tourism, the "going out" scale and development level of China's tourism enterprises will also be significantly improved.

1.1.7 Invigorating Tourism Through Science and Education: From Tactic to Strategic

Education and science constitute the basic support and continuous driving force for the development of the tourism industry. At the initial stage of China's reform and opening-up, the definition of the nature of tourism industry and the rapid development of inbound tourism produced a huge demand for tourism professionals especially when it came to the foreign-language tour guides and hotel managerial personnel who were extremely scarce. Therefore, developing tourism education and training professional talents had become an urgent need driven by the market. After the 1990s, the world has entered into the information age. With the settlement of shortage in tourism supply and the intensified competition from international market, China's tourism industry is gradually stepping into the buyer's market and a leapfrog development stage. Consequently, the main gap between China and the global tourism powers was mainly found in the domain of information technology and human resources. Entering the new century, "to invigorate tourism through science and education" and "to strengthen tourism with talents" has naturally become a strategic choice for the development of China's tourism industry.

China's tourism education system is mainly made up of college education and adult education. And its tourism college education can be divided into two levels, namely the secondary vocational education and the higher education, while its tourism adult education is carried out by tourism training centers and some tourism colleges. Since reform and opening-up over the past 40 years, driven both by the rapid growth of China's tourism industry and its education (mainly the higher education, secondary education and adult education), China's tourism education has become more and more mature. Through multiple levels of college education and various forms of in-service training, a large number of tourism professionals had been trained, vigorously supporting the development of the tourism industry.

In 1979, China's first tourism college was established in Shanghai, marking the beginning of China's tourism higher education. From 1980 on, the CNTA had subsidized eight domestic colleges in succession to set up tourism departments and tourism majors. Since then, alongside the reform on the educational system, more tourism colleges were established. In October 1978, China's first secondary vocational school of tourism was established in Jiangsu province. Thereafter, tourism schools were also established in Beijing, Hubei and Sichuan. At the beginning of China's reform and opening-up, tourism colleges and vocational technical secondary schools were just set up, which certainly could not satisfy the demand for talents in time and quantity, as a result, the tourism adult education emerged at that crucial moment. Taking the characteristics of the tourism industry into consideration, a training system made up by the national, provincial and municipal tourism departments together with tourism enterprises were gradually established and the tourism adult education was transformed from the "role of emergency handling" which it played in the very beginning into an important channel for tourism practitioners to improve their own competence. By 2007, the number of tourism colleges together with colleges or universities offering tourism department (major) had reached 770 in total, with nearly 400,000 students enrolled. There had also been 871 secondary vocational schools, with more than 370,000 students enrolled. The in-service trained personnel of the whole industry had exceeded 3.2 million. To select qualified guides, in 1989, the tour guide qualification examination was launched throughout the country. By the end of 2007, more than 580,000 people were holders of the tour guide qualification certificate, more than 400,000 people were holders of the tour guide IC card. Nearly 18,000 people obtained the intermediate tour guide certificate after passing relevant examinations (Figs. 1.6 and 1.7).

Tourism information is a bond that connects all links of the tourism industry. Information-based tourism in China started in the 1980s. With the entry of the foreign touristic hotel groups into the Chinese market, some foreign-funded and joint-venture hotels took the lead in applying computer technology. In 1981, China International Travel Service introduced the PRIME550 super small computer system from the US and in 1984, Shanghai Jinjiang Hotel introduced the computer management system developed by Conic Company of the US. Since then, the computer booking network system for airlines, the office automation system for tourism enterprises and other computer systems suitable for tourism enterprises have been gradually introduced.

In the 1990s, the development of the Internet brought about the full rising of tourism websites. In the new century, tourism e-commerce is booming rapidly, replacing some functions of traditional tourism enterprises and becoming a new force in the tourism industry. Websites with virtual tourism electronic map as the main service

Fig. 1.6 Shanghai institute of tourism

Fig. 1.7 Tour guide qualification certificate

keep emerging, and some cities in China have built three-dimensional urban tourism maps. Many tourism institutions is taking the advantage of Web2.0 era to explore deeper into the field of tourism information, leading to the creation of various service forms. It is safe to say that China's tourism industry has kept pace with the world in the application of new technologies in some aspects.

Apart from the construction of network management system and destination marketing system carried out by the tourism management departments at various levels, the "Golden Tourism Project" implemented under the auspices of the CNTA in 2000 also played an important role in promoting information-based tourism in China. Presently, more than 10 business management systems, including the star-rated hotel's management system, tourism complaint system, tourism statistics system, financial index management system of tourism, tourism project investment management system, scenic region (spot) management system, tour guide management, etc., have been established, which leading to the formation of a national tourism industry management system basically covering the management level of the whole industry. Furthermore, in 1997, the launching of China travel network (cntour.cn) had provided an important platform for the government to open its tourism affairs, publicize its tourism industry and release travel information.

1.2 Basic Understanding of the Development of China's Tourism in the Past Four Decades

1.2.1 China's Tourism in the Past 40 Years Is a Period of Constantly Deepening of the Understanding of Tourism and Gradual Grasping of the Law of Tourism

1.2.1.1 Nature of Tourism: From Business to Industry

Although this transformation was made with ease, the function of tourism had not been brought into full play. Even though some institutions had treated tourism as an industry, they considered it as a small business but not as a large one. In this transformation process, the tourism industry sought its own development by following the law of market operation and the law of industry development.

1.2.1.2 Tourism Market: From a Single Market to Three Large Markets

The tourism industry has completed the transformation from the single inbound tourism market to the three large markets of inbound, domestic and outbound tourism. During that process, profound changes took place in the understanding of the market. For example, in the past, the outbound tourism market had largely been neglected, but outbound tourism had promoted the generation of a series of tourism functions and the development and growth of travel agencies. It is also conducive for the international development and overseas expansion of China's tourism industry, thus needs to be re-recognized from a new perspective in the new era.

1.2.1.3 Tourism Demand: From Direct Demand to Derived Demand

Tourism demand was shifted from the former direct demands, such as sightseeing at the early stage to the latter coastal vacation, cultural experience, cross-country adventure and other demands in a series of aspects, which had promoted the creation of many new industries and the rapid development of the industry. In the meantime, the demands of different sub-industries have also been constantly extended during the process. For example, the catering sector had been extended from mere offering group dinner to a series of services, such as local flavor, specialty restaurant, themed dish, Western-style restaurant, dining experience, etc., which enabled the catering demand in tourism to get rid of the lower level of satisfying hunger.

1.2.1.4 Tourism Resources: From Traditional Resources to Comprehensive Utilization

The traditional tourism resource merely refers to the concept of sightseeing tourism, which involves the natural tourism resource and the humanistic tourism resource. However, the comprehensive utilization of the social resources is a new type of resource-based view, that is, to make use of all resources with tourism value to create a greater new value and added value. For example, the promotion of the industrial and agricultural tourism demonstration sites, namely—the combination of the traditional agricultural and industrial production resources and the market demands of the tourism industry, has achieved the goal of creating a larger social value.

1.2.1.5 Tourism Products: From Simple Sightseeing to Composite and Diversified Products

China's tourism products have been developed from purely sightseeing type to the diversified types of holiday leisure, specific tourism and other composite products, and from simply increasing the attraction of scenic spots to the comprehensive development of tourism destinations, thus conforming to the law of tourism development, promoting the in-depth development of tourism and mobilizing the enthusiasm of all parties involved.

1.2.1.6 Tourism Industry: From Small Tourism with Six Elements to Socialized Large Tourism

The tourism industry has gradually expanded from small tourism to socialized large tourism. The extension of the concept of tourism has further completed the nature and function of tourism, thus its overall significance for economic and social development can be more fully demonstrated.

1.2.1.7 Tourism Function: From Marginal Position to Central Mainstream

Tourism was often placed on the edge of national development strategies as an optional decoration, while the industry itself also believed that tourism could only play a marginal and supplementary role in economic and social development. However, there had been some misunderstandings therein, for in the process of development, tourism has become more active in integrating itself into the mainstream.

1.2.2 China's Tourism Industry Has Been Continuously Open for 40 Years

1.2.2.1 Tourism: A Pioneer of China's Opening-Up

Originating from inbound tourism, tourism is naturally open and, to some extent, a pioneer and promoter of China's opening-up. After China opened up to the outside world, foreigners came to China for sightseeing. These travellers were originally received by a subordinate organization of the ministry of foreign affairs. Later on, due to the entry of a large number of overseas tourists brought about by the opening-up policy, the reception was undertaken by a dedicated tourism bureau. Therefore in the beginning, tourism of China was generated from China's opening-up and served for opening-up in return. The opening-up has brought about tangible benefits to China and made its people more aware of their shortcomings. However, tourism is the earliest field of China that opened up to the outside world, and its demonstration effect on the opening-up policy cannot be ignored.

1.2.2.2 Interaction and Mutual Promotion of Tourism and Opening-Up

China's opening-up has promoted the development of its tourism while the latter in turn has advanced the opening-up in an all-round way. In other words, tourism has benefited from the opening-up and promoted the development of the opening-up. Tourism development and opening-up are precisely mutually promoted to a higher level.

1.2.2.3 Combination of Opening-Up to the Inside and Outside World

Opening-up to the outside world constitutes the internationalization of China's tourism while opening-up to the inside world constitutes the marketization of China's tourism. It can be said that at the early stage, China's opening-up focused on foreigners and foreign capital earnings, but due to the rapid development at the late stage and in the bid to seek the wellbeing of its own citizens and enterprises, it focused on establishing a unified national market. Moreover, after China's accession to the WTO, with the establishment of the national treatment policy, opening-up to domestic and international market will gradually be coordinated.

1.2.2.4 Combination of "Bringing-In" and "Going-Out"

At the early stage of development, tourism laid much more emphasis on the way of "bringing-in", which means attracting foreign tourists and foreign capital, technology, and management, etc. However, in the new era, with the implementation of the national strategy of going global, it is also the right time for Chinese tourists and tourism enterprises to go abroad, which will form a two-way interactive development pattern and promote the benign development of tourism.

1.2.3 The 40 Years of China's Tourism Is a Period Witnessing a Constant Acceleration of the Marketization Process

1.2.3.1 Opening-Up Promotes Marketization

After the opening up, the influx of overseas tourists naturally demanded that China, which was still in the closed planned economy, provide corresponding products and services according to the requirements of tourists. This process directly promoted the marketization of China, that is, tourism operation and business activities should be carried out in accordance with the requirements of market economy countries and international practices.

1.2.3.2 Supply Shortage Accelerates Marketization

At the early stage of China's tourism development, the supply shortage and short-term restriction seriously affected the image of China and the revenue of the tourism industry while the monopolistic management system also restricted the development of relevant industries. Therefore, a series of development measures taken afterwards were basically carried out towards the direction of marketization, that is, by virtue of the market force, the tourism industry has rapidly seen the increase of supply, the reduction of product shortcomings, the boost in the market competition and the improvement in the service quality.

1.2.3.3 Reform Promotes Marketization

The reform mentioned here refers not only to the policies from the state-level overall reform on the tourism industry, but also to the reform of the tourism industry itself. The reforms on tourism, from the state-owned enterprises to diversified ones, from product market to factor markets and from foreign-oriented service to comprehensive services, have always been accelerated under the impetus of various reform policies and measures.

1.2.4 The 40 Years of China's Tourism Is a Period Characterized by the Constant Exertion of the Tourism Industry's Comprehensive Functions

1.2.4.1 The Nine Functions of Tourism

The functions of China's tourism industry can be classified into nine aspects namely: The function of earning foreign exchange, the economic function, the social function, the ecological function, the cultural function, the diplomatic function, the function of poverty alleviation, the function of job enhancement and the function of education. The exertion of these tourism functions has made outstanding contributions to the promotion of economic and social development of China.

1.2.4.2 The Enhancement of the Comprehensive Functions

The development of China's tourism industry conforms to economic laws and social requirements, and the emphasis of tourism function in different periods is constantly changing. When China gets into the middle stage of industrialization, the comprehensive functions of tourism will become stronger and this will contribute to the evolution of the Chinese society towards the late stage of industrialization and the period of post-industrialization, and will equally promote the prosperity of the society as a whole.

1.2.5 The 40 Years of China's Tourism Is a Period Characterized by the Gradual Cultivation of the Concept of Tourism Development and Tourism Value

1.2.5.1 Concept of Tourism Development

After 40 years of development, China's tourism industry is kept on growing and maturing and its philosophy of development is more in line with the needs of future long-term development of the tourism industry itself.

Firstly, from single growth to development in an all-round way. To be specific, the tourism industry has been shifted from the single pursuit of inbound tourists and the increase of foreign exchange into the overall development of the industry. In fact, it has gone through the process from the single inbound tourism to the balanced coordinated development of inbound, domestic and outbound tourism. It has also gone through the process from quantity improvement to quality improvement and from extensive growth to intensive development.

Secondly, from the economic target to systematic targets. During the process of strengthening the industrial status of the tourism economy, emphasis was only laid on the economic index of the tourism industry. With the deepening of development, systematic targets have been set up for the tourism industry, including the economic target, the social target, the cultural target, the environmental target, the internationalization target and more scientific and comprehensive targets.

Third, from fair market to the harmonious development. The development of tourism itself is a process of promoting market fairness, increasing the marketization degree and constantly improving the market. In the process of the developing market economy, it is necessary to take into consideration the interests of all parties involved so as to achieve harmonious development.

Fourthly, from the people's livelihood to a pillar industry. From the perspective of scientific development, the tourism development shall be people-oriented, and at the same time, the tourism industry shall be a model industry to fully implement the people-oriented concept. The people-oriented concept aims to boost the national economy, and therefore to improve the people's livelihood.

Fifthly, sticking to environmental protection, cultural prosperity and sustainable development. In the process of developing its tourism industry, China has always given the top priority to environmental protection, cultural prosperity and the promotion of the sustainable development. Despite that there have been misunderstandings and verbal attacks in practice, the concept remains unshakable and which also can be considered as the root concept for tourism development.

1.2.5.2 The Values of Tourism

In the course of development, on the one hand, a new value system should be cultivated for the industry; on the other hand, it is necessary to help tourists construct their values in tourism.

For one thing, to be tourism enterprises with social responsibility should be advocated. The social responsibility of tourism enterprises lies in the following aspects: first, they should be responsible for the management of themselves; secondly, they should be responsible for the rights and interests of tourists; thirdly, they should be responsible for the public. To advocate corporate social responsibility is to guide tourism enterprises and business units to pay more attention to social and public interests in addition to their own interests, so as to jointly create a better harmonious and fairer development environment. And part of tourism's attributes as public goods is also gradually reflected, and its contribution to social welfare begins to emerge. For example, some tourism enterprises start to donate to public welfare, urban parks and museums throughout the country are open to the public for free, which in turn will boost the faster development of the tourism industry.

For another, to be tourists with social responsibility should be advocated. With China's economic and social development, the civic awareness, townsfolk consciousness and national consciousness of its people have been unceasingly intensified. In this process, a citizen's social responsibility also needs to be advocated, and to be a responsible tourist is an very important part of it. Being subjects of tourism behavior, a traveler's behavior does not only represent and demonstrate his or her own image but also the image of a whole nation. Therefore, greater attention should be paid to this aspect.

In essence, tourism values take people's interests as the starting point, quality of tourism as the benchmark requirement, civilized behavior as the basic element and the improvement of the quality of life as the fundamental purpose. In the new phase of tourism development, the development of new tourism values should be cultivated, and a new tourism value system should be constructed in China.

1.3 The Development Trend of China's Tourism Industry

1.3.1 The Division of Labor Among Travel Agencies Is Becoming More and More Specialized

Travel agencies were divided into those in charge of domestic business and those responsible for international business in the past. While in later development, the division of labor has become more detailed: different travel agencies can develop different tour routes, and travel agencies of the same brand can also develop different themed tourism and specialized tourism products. More so, there are more and more specialized intermediary companies, such as companies specialized in hotel reservation, ticket booking, restaurant reservation, tourist attraction booking, travel consultation, etc.

1.3.2 The Additional Services Provided by Tourism Agencies Are Becoming More and More Prominent

As customers become more and more picky and the competition becomes more and more fierce, tourism agencies pay more and more attention to the additional role of service in the process of serving customers in order to win over customers and enhance brand competitiveness. For example, though a professional service company focusing on providing tourists with hotel booking service, Beijing Golden Century has extended its services to ticket booking, car rent and pick-up services. The company cooperates with Agricultural Bank of China to provide financial services for customers and China Pacific Insurance Co., Ltd. to provide insurance guarantee services for customers, and it also cooperates with many other consumer units, such as catering and entertainment to provide discount entertainment and discount services for its members (customers).

1.3.3 Reservation Time Is Being Advanced

In the past, tourists were reluctant to make use of advanced booking services even when they were provided with such services by travel agencies and hotel booking companies as a consequence of tourists' consumption habit. However, thanks to the consumption guidance by tourism agencies, the booming of the holiday economy and the timely forecasting of the national macro information, tourists nowadays are paying more and more attention to booking in advance; otherwise, they may fail to get the service if their reservation comes late.

1.3.4 Tourism Services Are Constantly Innovated and Develop Towards Refinement

Guided by the relevant macro-policies of the state, and with the joint efforts of tourism intermediaries and relevant tourism departments, industrial tourism, agricultural tourism, forest tourism, ecological tourism and poverty-alleviation tourism will be gradually developed. Industrial tourism is a kind of tourist activity which tries to attract tourists by the process of industrial production, the appearance of factories and the display of industrial products. For example, the one-day industrial tourism project of "How the Steel Is Tempered" carried out by some steel industry production plants, including Shougang Group, Anshan Iron and Steel Group, Baosteel Group and so on has become a hot topic overnight. At the meantime, the agricultural tourism carried out in South Jiangsu has greatly promoted the development of agricultural economy. A typical example is the agricultural tourism project developed at Jianxinzhou of Nanjing. For the project, it is said that millions of kilograms of grapes produced there are sold to tourists on the spot annually, which can not only help to reduce transportation costs and losses, but can guarantee a good price. Therefore, this project alone has increased the income of local farmers by ten million yuan a year. In addition, the agricultural tourism projects are also flourishing in other parts of southern Jiangsu Province, such as at Hengshan Town of Changzhou, the high-tech agricultural park in Suzhou, the Dangui park of Kunshan, etc. (Fig. 1.8).

1.3.5 One-Day or Two-Day Tour to Outskirts Is Becoming More and More Popular

As Chinese people gradually get used to the Two-day Weekend system, tourism agencies start to take advantage of it by designing more and more short-term travel programs. Thus, more and more Chinese people tend to choose short-distance travel to outskirts rather than long-distance travel. As a result, one-day or two-day tour is becoming popular and more resorts have been set up. On weekends and during

Fig. 1.8 Agricultural tourism in Jianxinzhou of Nanjing

holidays or festivals, people travel to outskirts to enjoy peasants' meals, experience rural labor, appreciate landscape, and pursue a natural, fresh and unpretentious way of life. This can be proved by the fact that the growth index of domestic tourism is much higher than that of outbound tourism.

1.3.6 Self-Help Travel Is Becoming Fashionable

The traditional travel agency services have left a lot of negative impressions (mainly due to poor meals, poor accommodation and poor entertainment) on people and thus have made tourism become a trip with very little entertainment. However, due to the improved and convenient means of transportation, increasingly popularized private cars, prosperity and rapid development of hotel reservation companies, more and more Chinese people choose to travel by themselves and this has gradually become a trend. Especially during long holidays, it is not uncommon for three or five families to travel together, driving thousands of kilometers away from home, solving the accommodation problem by booking hotels through hotel reservation companies. What left for them to do is to arrange their trip as they like, so that the weaknesses of traditional travel agencies can be eradicated. In 2001 alone, the number of people using private cars as their means of transportation when going travelling was up to 15.7%.

1.3.7 Business Travel Is Becoming More and More Prominent

With the development of economy and trade, both domestic and international business travel are becoming more and more popular. According to statistics, there are 40 million business personnel of various types in China. Suppose each of them makes three business trips a year, the number of business tourists in China will reach 120 million and the number is increasing by millions each year. Business tourism also witnesses the trend of large-scale development, especially large business activities (including traditional and emerging business activities) are the main factors leading to the growth of business tourism. As can be seen from the composition proportion of the number of inbound tourists, 17.7% of them come for conference business, and 48.6% of the total number of tourists aged 25–44. Therefore, both travel agencies and the other emerging tourism agencies will attach great importance to the tourism business market.

1.3.8 The Futures-Form Tourism Has Sprouted Out

Although time-sharing holiday is a new form of tourism in China and it is still not standardized, more and more white-collar workers in cities will choose time-sharing holiday as long as 10, 20 and even 40 years. In 2001, the number of people who chose time-sharing holidays increased several times year on year, and it is estimated that more than 10,000 time-sharing holidaymakers will be purchased nationwide in the same year. At present, many travel agencies have been involved in futures-form tourism services to varying degrees, and several well-known travel agencies have joined hands to build resorts nationwide to carry out time-sharing vacation business.

1.3.9 Tourism Management Turns to Be Orderly and Standardized

Breakthrough progress has been made in the standardization of travel agencies in recent years. The fee charged by touristic attractions, tourism shopping, tips claimed by tour guides, etc. have been vigorously rectified and standardized, and a series of tourism policies and regulations have been issued. Moreover, in order to effectively regulate the behavior of tour guides, the two cards (chest card and score card) has been integrated into one, the new scoring method of nationwide networking has been implemented for tourist guide licenses, thus effectively restricting and standardizing the behaviors of tour guides, and pushing tourism agencies towards standardized management.

Fig. 1.9 China travel service head office

1.3.10 Chain Operation Is the General Trend of the Development of Tourism Intermediaries

Due to the virtual nature of tourism agencies, there are advantages and disadvantages as far as the development of chain management is concerned. However, the chain management of travel agencies is still under trial and construction. For example, China Travel Service Head Office has a unified brand name, having more than 200 domestic chain stores and 14 international chain stores; at present, China International Travel Service (CITS) has more than 160 sub-companies that use the same trade name; the newly-emerging company, China Comfort Travel (Conghui), is also using the same trade name. They operate independently and cooperate with each other in business, which is the primary form of chain stores (Fig. 1.9).

References

Lin F (2009) Research on the structure and adjustment of China's tourism industry. Available (online) http://www.ynta.gov.cn/Print.aspx?id=951, 10 Nov 2009

Project Group of China National Tourism Administration (2008) Research report on 40 years of reform and opening-up of China's tourism industry, Dec 2008

Song Z (2006) Research on China contemporary tourism development. Economic Management Press, Beijing

Chapter 2
Unconventional Development of China's Tourism Industry and Its Phases of Development

As mentioned earlier in Chap. 1, China's tourism industry started with the development of inbound tourism which in turn helped to promote the development of domestic tourism and outbound tourism. This mode of development was unconventional and government-dominated when compared to the tourism development mode of some developed Western countries in history. Judging from the Government's planning and management of tourism development and the scale of the above-mentioned three forms of tourism, China's tourism development went through a timely sequence. The inbound tourism was developed as the first priority and was successively followed by domestic tourism and outbound tourism, manifesting an unconventional development sequence.

2.1 Unconventional Development of China's Tourism Industry

2.1.1 Historical Inevitability of the Unconventional Development

As mentioned above earlier, China had taken a different mode from that of developed Western countries in the development of its tourism industry. Since the holding of the Third Plenary Session of the 11th Central Committee of the Communist Party of China[1] in 1978, China has begun to carry out the reform and opening-up policy, which paved the way for the development of its tourism industry. The year 1986 witnessed the implementation of China's "Seventh Five Year Plan" (1986–1990), a national

[1]The conference was a decisive turning point in post-1949 Chinese history, marking the beginning of the "Reform and opening-up" policy, and set China on the course for nationwide economic reforms.

© Social Sciences Academic Press and Springer Nature Singapore Pte Ltd. 2019

P. Zhou, *The Theory and Practice of China's Tourism Economy (1978–2017)*,
Research Series on the Chinese Dream and China's Development Path,
https://doi.org/10.1007/978-981-32-9107-2_2

plan aiming at the development of the country's economy and society. The Plan clearly stated that the tourism industry should be vigorously developed in order to increase the earning of foreign exchange. More so, it also stated that the construction of tourism cities and tourism areas should be strengthened, the cultivation of tourism talents, the production and sales of tourism commodity should be accelerated. In order to earn more foreign exchange, the Chinese government had to place the development of inbound tourism in the first place. Since then, the development of tourism industry had become a huge concern to the state. In the course of the vigorous development of inbound tourism, the development of domestic tourism also started gradually in China (Fig. 2.1).

In the "Eighth Five Year Plan" released in 1991, the tourism industry was even taken in the tertiary industry, and was to be vigorously developed to the same extent as finance, insurance, information technology, consulting, real estate and life service industry, etc. By 1995, the number of China's domestic tourists had reached 6.29 hundred million RMB and their total expenditure had reached 137.57 billion RMB, which certainly far outnumbered the international tourism receipts of 72.93 billion RMB and the number of inbound tourists of 46.39 million. Obviously, in terms of the total amount of tourists and tourism revenue, the domestic tourism market had begun to occupy a dominant position in the three major tourism markets. After 2000, the domestic tourism has been greatly boosted due to the policy support and the increase in the citizen's income brought about by the rapid economic growth. Therefore, the ranking of the tourism market in China had basically become stable in terms of revenue: with the domestic tourism coming first, the inbound tourism and the outbound tourism in the second and third place respectively.

Fig. 2.1 Third plenary session of the 11th Central Committee of the CPC

2.1.2 Analysis of the Characteristics of the Unconventional Development of the Tourism Industry in China

2.1.2.1 Inbound Tourism Had Become the Pilot for China's Tourism Development

Since the reform and opening-up in late 1978, with the influx of foreign tourists, China had witnessed a rapid development in international tourism with the incoming tourists as the main body. In 2009, China ranked fourth in the world Top 10 largest tourism destinations to receive international tourists, preceded by France, the United States and Spain successively. In terms of tourism receipts brought about by international tourists of the world's Top 10 destinations, China ranked fifth in the same year. If the number of overnight tourists and the receipts from inbound tourism can be used as two major indicators to measure a country's status of inbound tourism in the world, China had entered the world's Top Five.

The rapid growth of inbound tourism is not only reflected on the rapid increase in the number of incoming tourists and foreign exchange earnings, but also in the country's overall tourism development system worked out with the reception of incoming tourists as the focus.

Firstly, the regulation of the disproportionate development of inbound tourism had become the core for government's tourism management. Due to the influence of the political system, the specific management of all the issues relating to international tourism was a striking feature of China's tourism management in the period of the country's disproportionate development of its inbound tourism. All the issues in direct connection with tourism and incoming tourists, such as the approval of foreign-tourist-oriented attractions and places, the establishment and management of tourism service enterprises, and even the deciding of prices for foreign-related travel, etc., were brought under government control.

Secondly, catering for incoming tourists was the most prominent feature of tourism business service at that time. Regarding the service for inbound tourists, the number of tourist hotel and enterprises were expanding rapidly. More importantly, the management and service level of enterprises had undergone a qualitative leap, which is mainly reflected in the fact that China's tourist hotels are basically in line with international conventions due to the large number of inbound tourists. For instance, the authority of tourism had implemented a star rating system for hotels, whose purpose was to meet the needs of developing inbound tourism. Basically, most travel agencies were still engaged in incoming tourism services and the reception of international tourists (incoming tourists) was the main business for most travel agencies. It is safe to say that if there had been no inbound tourism business, there would have been no development of travel agency to its present level (Fig. 2.2).

Finally, the disproportionate development of inbound tourism had led to a change in understanding of tourism. The development of inbound tourism had helped to earn a certain amount of foreign exchanges for China's economic construction. At the same time, it had also led to the change in the Chinese government's and people's

Fig. 2.2 Badge for five-star hotels

understanding of tourism. It had become a consensus for people from all walks of life that the development of tourism could contribute to the promotion of social progress. In the process of the development of inbound tourism, the government had accumulated certain experiences in standardization and management of its tourism industry. The management skills for tourism service had been improved, and the general public's understanding of tourism had been greatly elevated, which had both contributed to lay a foundation for the all-round development of the tourism industry in China.

2.1.2.2 Strict Control of Outbound Tourism, and Heavy Dependence on Overseas Tourism Markets at the Early Stage

Due to the fact that outbound tourism required the consumption of a large amount of foreign exchanges, it was under strict control by the Chinese government in the beginning. In the 1980s, the personnel going out for official business constituted the absolute majority of outgoing tourists. Before the 1980s, the number of people going out for official business was relatively small, yet since the reform and opening-up, with the expansion of foreign exchanges, the number increased dramatically. In a fairly long period of time, the tourism consumption triggered by outgoing official business had constituted the main part of China's outbound tourism.

The development of inbound tourism in advance had contributed to the creation of China's tourism industry. To a certain extent, at the early stage of China's tourism development, the inbound tourism was equivalent to China's tourism industry as a whole, and the domestic tourism enterprises' dependence on the overseas tourism markets was absolute. Once there was a market fluctuation, China's tourism market would be inevitably and seriously affected. There is no doubt that, besides depending on China's Hong Kong and Taiwan districts and the overseas Chinese, China had to largely rely on Japan, the United States and the Western European countries as the main source markets for incoming tourism, which, of course, was the only choice for the Chinese people at that time and there was no other alternative. In order to attract tourists from the neighboring countries, such as Mongolia, Korea, Vietnam, India, Nepal, Pakistan, Afghanistan, etc., and in order to tap new tourism markets, it was not only necessary to do more promotion, but to depend on the economic and social development and progress of those countries which undoubtedly, necessitated a long-term process. This implies that, the diversification of the inbound tourism market in China could not be accomplished overnight.

From the history of China's tourism development, according to relevant tourism statistics, since the 1950s, there had been three forms of tourism more or less in China, namely, the inbound tourism, the outbound tourism and the domestic tourism. However, the development of inbound tourism had long been the focus by the Chinese government. The development of inbound tourism was a kind of overt development which was highlighted, and the development of domestic tourism was a kind of covert development which was neglected and the outbound tourism was even considered somewhat "illegal". As mentioned above, China's tourism development followed an unconventional development sequence, with the development of inbound tourism in the first place, the domestic tourism and outbound tourism in the second and third.

2.1.2.3 The Binary Structure of China's International Tourism and Domestic Tourism

In terms of consumer spending, there was a big gap between China's inbound tourism and domestic tourism services. According to statistics in 1999, the per capita expenditure of foreign tourists to China was about 1012 US dollars; As for domestic tourism, the per capita expenditure was 394 RMB, and the urban tourists' expenditure was 614.8 yuan, and the rural tourists' expenditure was 249.5 yuan. It can be clearly seen that the gap of the per capita expenditure between inbound tourists and domestic tourists is huge. Even after the deduction of long distance transportation expense of 33.1% from the total, the per capita expenditure of inbound tourists was still ten times more than that of domestic tourists. The huge gap imposed a big challenge to the government and enterprises in management. As a result of this, China's domestic tourism and international tourism (mainly inbound tourism) has become two independent markets, thus the binary economic structure came into being. Moreover, owing to the different policies adopted by the government on international tourism and domestic tourism, the binary structure was institutionally strengthened.

Researches show that in order to transform a binary economic system into to a dual system, efforts should not be spared in promoting the service industry and the improvement of urbanization from the aspects of technology and institution, so as to advance the evolution of division of labor. Decided by the characteristics of the tourism industry, the elimination of the binary structure calls not only for the development of related industries and social economy, but also for the adjustments of relevant policies made by the government.

2.1.2.4 The International Tourism Bore a Heavy Responsibility for Politics and Economy

Since the founding of the People's Republic of China, international tourism has been a part of the political work of the state, and its purpose is to meet the needs of foreign political exchanges. In the course of receiving inbound tourists, major attention was paid to raise the political influence of the state, and to publicize China's achievements in socialist construction from every aspect. Compared to inbound tourism, the outbound tourism then carried a much stronger political color. For the purpose of fulfilling certain political tasks, people sent abroad had to undergo stringent checks, their destinations were carefully selected, and their activities abroad were strictly guided. Under the pressure of such a heavy political task, China's outbound tourism before 1978 had obviously deviated from its original meaning of existence.

After the reform and opening-up, apart from some special activities, the original political color of China's outbound tourism gradually faded. In a general sense, it no longer assumed the duty of political reception and publicity. However, the influence of the political factors in the development of outbound tourism still remains essential. Be it inbound tourism or outbound tourism, a sound political relation between nations has always been a significant and basic condition for inter-nation tourism requires inter-governmental cooperation and promotion. Scholars have aired out their views on the importance of tourism in their researches. Some hold that "tourism is essential for the establishment and improvement of political relations among different nations", and "tourism can help to enhance national integrity, international understanding, friendship and peace"; some even believe that international tourism is a fundamental approach for international cooperation, and China's opening-up to the West and its development of international tourism in the late 1970s is such a good example.

At the beginning stage of the reform and opening-up, being an important means for earning foreign exchange, China's inbound tourism had to take up the important responsibility of boosting economy. Earning foreign exchange had become the primary and the core purpose for China to develop its international tourism, and how to gain more foreign exchange had been the focus for the government to manage the tourism industry. In order to fulfill this task and to vigorously develop inbound tourism, the strict control of outbound tourism had become the major policy for China's tourism development.

Presently, China has huge foreign exchange reserves, reaching 609.9 billion US dollars by the end of 2004 and it keeps on growing. With the development of economy and the improvement of people's living standard, China witnessed the rapid growth of its outbound tourism. Under such a condition, some researchers proposed that the outbound tourism should be "channeled" rather than "blocked". In order to have a correct understanding of the significance of outbound tourism, it is necessary for China to re-examine its fundamental policies for tourism development. In the meanwhile, some people think that China's outbound tourism is growing too fast, if there is no intervention, it will exert a huge influence on China's international balance of payments. And the huge "leakage" of domestic demand will dramatically affect China's ultimate consumption; therefore, special attention should be paid to it. From this point of view, the concept of earning foreign exchange by tourism is still deeply rooted in some people's mind.

2.2 Analysis of China's Tourism Developmental Phases

A survey of the development of the tourism industry since China's reform and opening-up, its phases can be roughly divided into four stages: (1) the primary stage for tourism development (1978–1984); (2) the nurturing stage for the tourism industry (1985–1991); (3) the stage for elevating the status of the tourism industry (1992–1998); (4) the expansion stage for the tourism industry (1999–present).

2.2.1 *The Primary Stage for Tourism Development (1978–1984)*

The period (from 1978 to 1984) was both the initial stage for China to switch from the planned economy to the market economy, and also the period for China's tourism industry to sprout up under the planned economy. In the beginning of reform and opening-up, Deng Xiaoping, the architect of China's reform and opening-up expressed his views on the development China's tourism industry in three of his important speeches delivered in 1979, and the essence of which is about creating opportunities to develop tourism, so as to promote the growth of the national economy. In the beginning stage of the tourism industry, the important speeches made by Deng Xiaoping produced a direct driving force for the development of the nation's tourism industry, and also provided a theoretical and institutional basis for the development of China's tourism industry. Since then, a sound policy environment had gradually emerged to support the tourism industry in the whole nation.

2.2.1.1 The Historical Change in the Tourism Administrative System

In 1978, the CPC Central Committee approved of a tourism-development report issued by the Ministry of Foreign Affairs and within the same year a new tourism administrative system was established. It was clearly stated in the government report that China Travel and Sightseeing Bureau (founded in 1964) was directly under the State Council and that tourism bureaus of the provincial level should be set up to manage local tourism affairs, and the scope of their administrative power was also classified. In 1982, the name of China Travel and Sightseeing Bureau was officially changed to China National Tourism Administration. Thus, it had become a new independent institution of administration and management, responsible for guiding and managing the nation's tourism. Correspondingly, most provinces had also set up tourism administrative institutions to deal with tourism-related affairs. This historic change of China's tourism administration system marked the transformation of China's tourism from a reception service authorized by the state to an economic industry contributing to the whole national economy. Moreover, the change of the system also manifested the nation's true understanding of the nature of tourism, which therefore contributed to re-establishment of the historical status of China's tourism industry. Since then, China's tourism began to develop as an independent economic industry.

2.2.1.2 The Change of Market Management Pattern

Based on the tourism administrative system, China's tourism industry started to grow within the framework of the planned economic system through the exploitation of the market mechanism; this was done through the mobilization of all social resources available to accelerate the development of the tourism industry. Within the period, the central government had timely put forward the policy of "Five Changes" and "Five Together", which means the change: (1) from developing inbound tourism only to the joint development of the inbound tourism and the domestic tourism, (2) from mainly engaging in tourism reception to the exploitation and construction of tourism resources together with the tourism reception, (3) from merely depending on national investment in the construction of tourism facilities to the attraction of individual, departments, collectivities, and local investment, (4) from merely relying on domestic investment to the use of domestic investment together with foreign capital, and (5) from regarding tourism institutions as state-run only to enterprises run on commercial basis. With the implementation of the policy, China's tourism industry forged ahead to the market management characterized by "unified leadership, decentralized management, separation of enterprise from administration", which greatly triggered off the enthusiasm of people from various sectors to the development of the tourism industry. Thus, it had become one of the most important policies for China to develop its tourism industry at the primary stage. Having gone through the primary stage of development, the market management system of the tourism industry also began to be set up in China, thus the nation's tourism had entered into the stage of market economy.

2.2.2 *The Nurturing Stage of the Tourism Industry (1985–1991)*

The nurturing stage of China's tourism industry lasted from 1985 to 1991. During this period, the nation's policy for tourism development was further clarified, and the means for the management of tourism market was constantly improved. In the late 1980s most especially, various policies and measures for the promotion of the tourism industry market were issued continually, and the market-regulation means for the boosting of the coordinated development of the tourism industry were also established gradually in China. The tourism industry grew rapidly due to the impetus of the overseas demand, leading to a bigger tourism scale. And the construction of infrastructures for tourism was constantly improving, and the six elements including food and beverage, accommodation, transportation, sightseeing, shopping and entertainment were basically improved. With the continuous improvement of reception capacity, tourism attractions and scenic spots gradually became more and more mature, a large number of hot tourist cities emerged rapidly, and the scale of the tourism market continued to expand. Therefore, this period was the first period which saw the rapid development of China's tourism industry.

2.2.2.1 The Importance of the Tourism Industry Began to Be Recognized

In April 1986, in the Seventh Five Year Plan (1986–1990) approved by the National People's Congress, it was clearly stated that the tourism industry should be vigorously developed so as to increase the earning of foreign exchange, and to promote friendly exchanges between peoples from all over the world. This was the very first time that tourism was officially absorbed in the national plan.

2.2.2.2 The Management of the Tourism Industry Became Standard

During the period, a series of laws and regulations concerning tourism were issued; the management system for the tourism industry was basically shaped; regulations, management measures and the corresponding national standards for different industries were promulgated, and tourism management was separated from the planned-economy mode to a standard one. For example, concerning the management of international tourism hotels, in 1988, the CNTA issued concrete regulations concerning the assessment of star ratings for international tourism hotels, which was the first step taken by the hotel industry towards standardized management. This therefore paved the way for China's international tourism hotels to quickly adapt themselves to the international standards especially at the level of hardware construction and service quality. This made China's hotel industry one of the pioneer domestic industries that had met the international standard.

Concerning the management of travel agencies, in 1988, the CNTA also formulated interim regulations for the administration of its travel agencies. According to these regulations, detailed clauses such as scope of business, etc. were all stipulated for all types of travel agencies to satisfy the examination and approval procedures, and the management measures, etc. From the period on, there had been rules for the approval and management of all types of travel agencies, which laid a foundation for the standardization of the tourism market.

2.2.2.3 The Marketing Concept of Tourism Was Gradually Established. In the Course of the Development of the Tourism Industry, the Market Concept Was Improved

With the growing scale of the tourism industry, the concept of considering tourism as an economic industry had been further enhanced, and the concept of promoting the market management of tourism had become clearer. In terms of tourism management, the first concern was laid on the market demand, and competition was based on the improvement of service quality and sales promotion; meanwhile, more attention was paid to the improvement of the image of touristic attractions and touristic cities. In

1988, the activity of the "Travel in the Year of the Dragon"[2] launched in Beijing pioneered China's tourism promotion campaign, therefore making this period an epoch-making one in China's tourism promotion (Fig. 2.3).

In brief, the period from 1978 to 1991 was not only a time when the reform on China's economic system was deepening, but also a period when China's tourism industry was sprouting up from the planned economic system, and the continuous breaking through the barriers of the planned economy to win more space for the development of the industry. More detailedly, firstly, a national institution of tourism administration was set up so that authority was given to the management of the industry, and a top-down management of the whole industry was implemented, endowing the tourism industry with the characteristic of independent development. Secondly, tourism roles were separated from the original duty of receiving foreign tourists, and it became an independent economic industry for development; meanwhile, after getting rid of the position subservient to politics, it had gained economic space for independent development. Thirdly, based on the characteristics resulting from the development of the tourism industry, a series of rules and regulations for the management of the industry were formulated, which ensured rapid and healthy development of China's tourism industry in its initial stage. After ten years of exploration, a management system which is market-oriented and suitable for China's tourism industry finally came into existence, and China's tourism industry entered into a new stage.

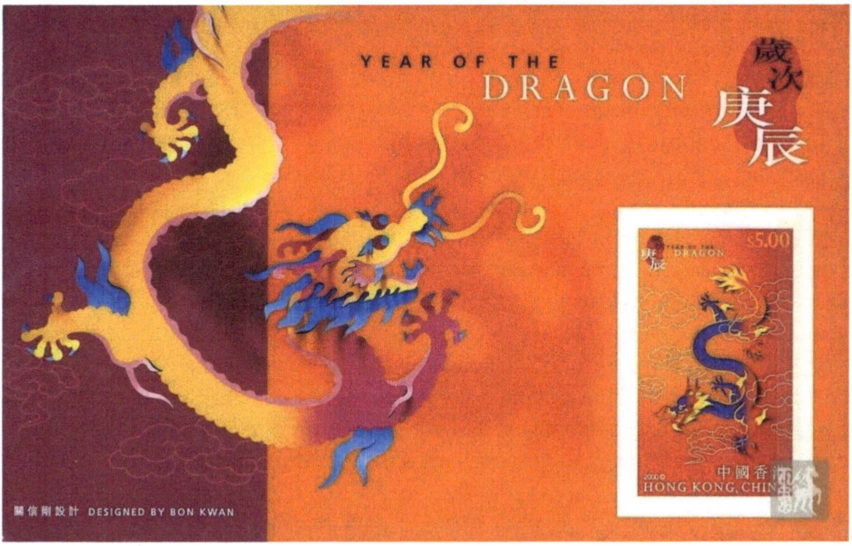

Fig. 2.3 The Year of Dragon

[2]The Year of the Dragon, the dragon is one of the 12-year cycle of animals which appear in the Chinese zodiac related to the Chinese calendar, and it is the only animal that is termed 'legendary'. The Dragon is the fifth sign in the Chinese Horoscope and signifies luck.

2.2.3 The Stage of Elevating the Status of the Tourism Industry (1992–1998)

From 1992 to 1992, with the establishment of the national market economy, the tourism industry moved from the beginning stage to the stage of further growth. During this stage, (1) new development was achieved in the tourism industry, the position of the tourism industry was further elevated, and the industrial system of tourism was basically made; (2) tourism reception capacity and reception scale grew side by side, and the scale of the tourism industry expanded steadily; (3) a relatively standard management system was established and specific measures were taken constantly to address problems in the tourism market; (4) tourism products evolved from sightseeing alone to a diversified sightseeing, vacationing, and other specific items, and country-level tourist resorts were launched; (5) market demand grew rapidly, especially, the domestic tourism had gradually dominated the tourism industry. During this stage, having successfully completed the transformation of its developmental stage, China's tourism industry has leaped onto a new stage, thus further manifesting itself as a sunrise industry.

2.2.3.1 The Tourism Industry Was Confirmed as a New Growth Point for National Economy

With the development of the tourism industry and its continuous contribution to the national economy, its role of being a new growth point for national economy has become increasingly prominent. In the "Decision on Accelerating the Development of the Third Industry" formulated by the CPC Central Committee and the State Council in 1992, the tourism industry was for the first time listed as one of the key industries among the third class industries. In 1998, at the Central Economic Work Conference held in December, the tourism industry was identified as a new growth point for national economy due to the formidable strength that the industry possesses, including its broad market prospects, international competitiveness, strong connection with other industries, more employment opportunities that it provides, and its role for promoting the balanced development of regional economy, etc. At the same time, all provinces, autonomous regions and municipalities throughout the country were trying their best to build the tourism industry as a pillar and a leading industry, which greatly strengthened the "government-dominated" efforts in the development of the industry. By the end of 20th Century, the scale of China's international tourism had greatly expanded, and its status had been significantly improved globally. Judging both from the number of inbound tourists and the earning of foreign exchanges, China has been one of the biggest tourism destinations in the world, and the tourism industry's contribution to the national economy has also greatly increased. According to the data released by the CNTA, the country's total tourism revenue contributed to 4.32% of the total GDP in 1998.

2.2.3.2 The Overall Development of Domestic Tourism

In order to meet the republic's increasingly growing needs for domestic travel, in 1993, the CNTA clearly stated in the "Opinions on the Positive Development of Domestic Tourism" that: (1) the domestic tourism industry should be included in the plans for the development of the national economy and society; (2) a unified domestic tourism market which is equally open and fair in competition should be established; (3) service products of mass tourism should be vigorously developed; (4) the service quality of domestic tourism should be improved so as to safeguard tourists' rights and interests. At the same time, it is proposed that tourism administrative departments, together with other relevant departments, should gradually establish service quality standards for transportation, sightseeing, accommodation, food, shopping, entertainment and so on; and (5) moral education ought to be strengthened so as to improve service quality of tourism practitioners. The release of the document marked the formal integration of the domestic tourism industry into the management of the tourism industry, and since then, domestic tourism has begun to play an important role in China.

At the same time, outbound travel, which is another travel demand from the public, began to attract the government's attention. In 1990, the CNTA officially started up the overseas tourism markets for Chinese citizens to visit at their own expense. And in order to further standardize the management of outbound tourism, in 1997, the State Council approved of the interim measures for the management of Chinese citizens traveling abroad at their own expense. Therefore, many countries and regions perceived the huge profit in attracting Chinese travellers. Hongkong, Macao and Singapore, Malaysia and Thailand, some other countries in the Asia-Pacific region, such as Australia, New Zealand, South Korea, Japan, etc. were also considered as Chinese citizens' outbound-travel destination countries and regions by the Chinese government. Up till then, China's tourism industry had become gradually complete, and its national tourism witnessed an overall development.

2.2.3.3 The Commercialized Management of the Tourism-Industry Market Was Accelerated

Under the guidance document for accelerating the development of the tertiary industry ratified by the CPC Central Committee and the State Council in 1992, the macro management of the tourism market was strengthened; a management system oriented towards the tourism industry was established; the directives for the development of the industry was coordinated and guided under the market means, the industry regulations and quality standards. Concerning the promotion of the tourism market, the state administration of tourism proposed a "five-year promotion plan (1993–1997)". With the aim of regulating the tourism market, a series of measures for the management of the industry were formulated, and a variety of industry standards were launched. In 1993, standards for the tourism industry involving the management of tourism services, and tourism service facilities, etc. were clearly stated by the State

Bureau of Technical Supervision. The quality guarantee system for travel agencies was introduced in 1994. In the domain of structural adjustment, an industrial management mechanism characterized by the certification of subject qualification of the tourism market as well as the guidance of market behavior, initially took shape. In 1996, the State Council issued the "Regulations on Administration of Travel Agencies". Thereafter, the annual inspection system for all kinds of travel agencies was implemented. New market guidance was adopted to guide tourism hotels and other industries with obvious characteristics of enterprises, while the traditional administrative measures were gradually abandoned. Moreover, with the acceleration of the course of marketization of the tourism industry, the pace was quickened for China to adapt its tourism industry to the market economy.

2.2.3.4 The Tourism Product Structure and Market Structure Were Diversified

In the 1990s, China's tourism products became diversified. More attention was paid to the in-depth development of the traditional tourism spots mainly involving landscape, cultural relics, folk customs and so on. Holiday tourism spots became more and more popular. The original resorts have begun to adjust their target markets and products. Centering on the state-level and the provincial-level resorts, they had developed a group of touristic spots within the country for tourists on vacation, thus leading to the emergence of a batch of tourist resorts (or bands) around cities. The rise and prosperity of the in-depth development of sightseeing destinations and holiday tourism destinations were the basic characteristics of this period. Some of the new tourism types, such as forest tour, green tour, scientific research tour, urban and rural tour, business tour, study tour and so on had all gone through considerable development. With the development of China's economy and society as well as the adjustment of its international relations, the structure of China's international tourism market had also undergone significant changes, manifested by the huge expansion of regional market shares and the transformation of the surrounding countries and regions into major tourism destinations. During this period, domestic tourism was boosted wholly, while outbound tourism was at the threshold of huge development, and the further relaxation of policies brought about a new breakthrough in its development.

2.2.4 The Expansion Stage for the Tourism Industry (1999–Present)

Since the late 1990s, with the gradual deepening of China's market economic system, there arose a new trend in the development of the tourism industry: the status of the tourism industry was established; the formation of the concept of "big tourism, big market, big product, and big industry" led to a big breakthrough against the traditional concept of considering tourism as a subordinate industry; the image of tourism became more prominent, and its positioning became more obvious; the reform on tourism enterprises was continually deepened, and the modern enterprise system for tourism was gradually established; the pressure from the economic globalization continued to increase, that is, more foreign capitals, management skills, and technologies entered into various sectors of the tourism industry, and the domestic tourism enterprises faced a double competition from both home and abroad. The development of domestic tourism stimulated national consumption, which in turn helped to expand the domestic demand to a larger extent. As a new growth point of China's economy, tourism had obviously played a role in the development of its local and regional economy as well as the entire economy.

2.2.4.1 The Status of the Tourism Industry Was Established in the Regional Economy

The vigorous development of domestic tourism greatly stimulated the enthusiasm of local governments to develop the tourism industry, especially in China's central and western regions and economically less developed areas, in which the advantages of local tourism resources were re-examined, and the tourism industry was considered as an important industry for the promotion of the local economy. For example, in Chongqing municipality and Sichuan province, tourism was positioned as a new economic pillar industry; Jilin province strove to build tourism into a major economic industry, or a key industry in the tertiary industry; Inner Mongolia endeavored to practically list out the tourism industry as the leading industry in the tertiary industry, or rather as an effective industry to improve the people's quality of life and to alleviate poverty.

Admittedly, in those areas, there is still a long way to go before the actual realization of their planned goals for tourism development; therefore, more painstaking efforts and more time are needed. However, the whole society has reached a consensus in considering the tourism industry as a new economic growth point for the national economy, and the consensus is also echoed with full recognition and support from local governments, and concrete actions have been taken by them as well.

2.2.4.2 The Management of the Industry Was Strengthened by Local Governments

The tourism industry is a comprehensive industry involving many domains in the national economy, characterized by its high degree of marketization and difficulty of management. In order to standardize the market order, ensure the healthy and orderly development of the tourism industry, besides the relevant laws, regulations and standards formulated by the central government, local governments have also released a series of local laws and regulations to strengthen the management of the tourism industry. Altogether 16 provinces, autonomous regions, and municipalities, such as Henan, Hebei, Shandong, Anhui and Tibet, etc. issued their own local regulations on the administration of tourism, and two other provinces and one municipality, namely, Guizhou, Heilongjiang, and Tianjin, released their regulations and measures on the administration of the tourism industry. In addition, in order to standardize the market order, straighten out the management system of the industry, some local governments successively promulgated specific local regulations to intensify the coordination and management of the tourism industry. In order to promote the development of the tourism industry, local governments at all levels started out by sorting out the management system, determining goals and direction for market regulation, and clarifying focal points for their future work.

2.2.4.3 The Vigorous Development of Outbound Tourism

In July 1997, the State Council approved of the interim measures for the management of Chinese citizens traveling abroad at their own expense. The promulgation and implementation of the administrative measures marked the transition from the pilot stage to the formal implementation stage of China's self-funded overseas tourism. By adopting the managing measures, the state aimed to regulate the behavior of its citizens traveling abroad, and at the same time, visits to Hong Kong and Macao, as well as border travel and outbound travel were all taken into unified management. Outbound tourism is an important index reflecting a country's degree of openness to the outside world, and also a symbol indicating the developmental stage of a country's economy. Outbound tourism is also an index which shows to what level a nation's living standards has reached. Although China's outbound tourism is far from completely open, it is constantly forging ahead. From 1991 to 1997, the average growth rate of the number of outbound tourists increased by 17.25% annually; from 1997 to 2000, the average annual growth rate increased by 30%, showing a very sound momentum in the development of outbound travel. In order to satisfy its citizens' increasing desire for outbound travel and meet the continuous demands for international tourism cooperation, the number of outbound tourism destinations designated by the Chinese government is continuously increasing. By the end of 2001, the number of outbound tourism destinations confirmed by the Chinese government had reached 20, including countries and regions like Singapore, Malaysia, Thailand, and China's Hong Kong and Macao Special Administrative Regions, etc. With the change of various factors, namely, the increase in China's foreign exchange reserves, the changes in foreign trade situations, the increasing demand for outbound travel, China's accession to the WTO, some countries' elimination of visa discrimination against Chinese nationals, and the growing efforts on the promotion of their tourism products by international communities, the Chinese government will further relax its policies on outbound tourism.

Fig. 2.4 5-leaf, the highest level of green hotel in China

2.2.4.4 The Gradual Recognition of the Sustainable Development of the Tourism Industry

Sustainable development strategy is the basic strategy of China's social and economic development and this strategy should be implemented by other industries for effective development. Hence, it is by no means a quick fix or a marketing gimmick. It is safe to say that there is a natural coupling relationship between the tourism industry and sustainable development. The sustainable development of the tourism industry is not only an indispensable part of the country's overall strategy for the sustainable development of its whole economy, but is also a necessity for the development of the tourism industry itself. It is widely accepted by the tourism industry that if there is no real sense of sound environmental and sustainable social development, the sustainable development of the industry will be out of the question. In recent years, the tourism industry has gained a certain understanding of sustainable development and great progress has been made in some industries and places. The activity of building green hotel in Zhejiang province has opened up a road for the sustainable development of China's hotel industry, created experience and promoted the green operation and green marketing activities of the national hotel industry. Moreover, in the course of applying for world cultural and natural heritage, the awareness of sustainable tourism development has been enhanced. Of course, the sustainable tourism development is by no means a short-term goal, and cannot be accomplished within a short period of time (Fig. 2.4).

History has proven that marketization is not only a prerequisite for tourism development, but a necessity to ensure the further development of the tourism industry in China. After 20 years of development, China's tourism industry has reached a certain scale, and has gradually stepped onto a normal development track. Both the government and the industry have accumulated some experiences, and they are fully aware of the gap between China and the world tourism powers. They have also learned to deal with the new situation—the quickened pace of economic globalization and the ever-changing domestic and foreign demand for tourism. Thus, China's tourism industry is growing bigger and stronger under the increasingly fierce competition from home and abroad.

Chapter 3
Structure of Industrial Tourism and Diversified Development of Tourism Products in China

By 2010, the total revenue of China's tourism was 1.44 trillion RMB and 11.5 million people were engaged in the tourism industry. In the same year, China's domestic tourists reached 2.15 billion persons and the receipts of domestic tourism reached 1.15 trillion RMB. The tourism rate of its residents of the year was 1.4 persons. Due to the reform and opening-up in the past four decades, the structure of China's tourism industry has also undergone great changes.

3.1 Analysis of Characteristics and Advantages of China's Tourism Resources

3.1.1 Types of China's Tourism Resources

Tourism resources are the basis of tourism development. The so-called tourism resources refer to the things or the natural factors existing in a society which appeal to tourists; which can stimulate tourists' travel motivation; which has a certain tourism function and value; which can be exploited and used by the tourism industry and which can produce economic benefits, social benefits and environmental benefits, etc.

Concerning the classification of tourism resources, the most commonly used method is the dichotomy method. In accordance with its basic attributes (or contributing factors), tourism resources can be divided into two types: the natural tourism resources and the cultural tourism resources. With the deepening of understanding, some scholars also divided tourism resources into three types according to their attributes: the natural tourism resources, the cultural tourism resources and the social resources. Some even divided tourism resources into four types still based on their attributes: the natural resources, the historic resources, the social resources and the modern artificial attractions. These different means of classification are expanding

© Social Sciences Academic Press and Springer Nature Singapore Pte Ltd. 2019

P. Zhou, *The Theory and Practice of China's Tourism Economy (1978–2017)*,
Research Series on the Chinese Dream and China's Development Path,
https://doi.org/10.1007/978-981-32-9107-2_3

and researches in tourism resources especially in the macro aspect have significant effects on further development and utilization of tourism resources and tourism products.

3.1.2 Characteristics of China's Tourism Resources

The basic characteristics of China's tourism resources can be summarized into four aspects: diversity, uniqueness, antiquity and richness.

The so-called "diversity" means China's tourism resources are of various types and multiple functions. All types of resources used for the development of tourism by other countries or regions in the world can be found in China. For example, China is rich in beautiful scenery and picturesque landscapes. In China, tourists can find whatever they want to visit, such as grand plateaus, rolling mountains, deep canyons, amazing caves, beautiful hills, boundless basins and plains, which are all dazzlingly charming to all visitors.

The so-called "uniqueness" means China boasts of many unique tourism resources. For example, China is endowed with unique landscapes, rare animals and plants, ancient architectures, splendid cultures and arts, etc. The peculiar tourism resources of China are not only of unique types but are also large in amount, which are extremely appealing to travelers (Fig. 3.1).

The so-called "antiquity" means there are a lot of historical heritages in China. As one of the cradles of human civilization, China enjoys a long history and splendid culture. Thus, its historical and cultural resources occupy a very important place in the nation's whole tourism resources.

Concerning the so-called "richness", many researchers think that China's tourism resources are not only rich in variety but also profound in culture. The rich resources makes China rank among the top of the world's resources.

3.1.3 Advantages of China's Tourism Resources

The tourism development of a country or region should be based on its local tourism resources. For the sake of the development of international tourism when competing with other countries, it is necessary for the Chinese people to analyze the distinctive advantages of tourism resources. It is only by giving full play to the advantages of its unique resources that China will be able to make more progress in the development of its international tourism.

It is undoubtedly true that China is abundant in tourism resources. In order to produce a qualitative leap in the tourism industry, people have to seek for the distinctive advantages of their tourism resources, especially in developing the inbound tourism. For example, China possesses a lot of summer resorts, winter ski resorts, sunshine, beaches and seas, but the advantages of these tourism resources are not outstanding when compared with the surrounding countries. If China wants to develop its

Fig. 3.1 A Lovely Panda

international tourism, it has to rely on the tourism resources which have advantages beyond comparison. The same is true for different regions in a country: if a region wants to develop local tourism, it should also seek comparative advantages of tourism resources.

The comparative advantages of China's tourism resources mainly lie in two aspects: one is the diversified and unique natural resources; the other is its rich and colorful cultural resources. The advantages of China's natural tourism resources are mainly derived from its vast territory as well as the diversity and uniqueness of its geology and weather conditions. The most important comparative advantage of China's tourism development is the advantage in human resources.

Cultural factors will play an increasingly important role in tourism competition, in other words, the attraction of a tourism destination mainly comes from its peculiar cultural features and this a view widely accepted by the world academic circle of tourism. According to relevant researches, the number of foreign tourists coming to China for sightseeing is quite large, among whom the majority want to experience the cultural resources in China, particularly the famous cultural relics and historic sites. For example, many tourists consider the Great Wall of China[1] as the symbol

[1]The Great Wall of China, first built 2000 years ago and being one of the seven wonders of the world, is a series of fortifications made of stone, brick, tamped earth, wood, and other materials, generally built along an east-to-west line across the historical northern borders of China to protect the Chinese states and empires against the raids and invasions of other various ethnic groups or states.

Fig. 3.2 The Badaling great wall in Beijing

of the Chinese nation; therefore, the Great Wall is a touristic site which can never be neglected by most foreign tourists. After the Badaling Great Wall[2] was opened in 1981, it had received more than 90 million tourists, including 320 state leaders, which clearly proves the significant market appeal for traditional cultures (Fig. 3.2).

3.2 Analysis of the Industrial Structure of China's Tourism

Although China's tourism industry started late, its industrial structure has undergone remarkable changes in the past 40 years of rapid development. Its industrial structure developed from merely a single travel agency industry into a complete industry with catering, accommodation, transportation, sightseeing, shopping and entertainment service, etc., and a larger size of an industrial scale also came into being. However, it is also quite clear that China's tourism industry is still at its initial stage of industrial development and therefore immature. Its industrial scale and output is of a low level. China's tourism industry is at a low level in both its industrial scale and its benefits, especially the benefits of the tourism industry is obviously lagging behind its scale expansion.

[2]The Badaling Great Wall, is located in Yanqing County, 70 km north of Beijing city. In ancient time, Badaling Great Wall is a very important pass to protect Beijing City on the north side, with the name of the Key to the North Gate of Beijing city. It is the site of the most visited section of the Great Wall partly because it is close to Beijing city and connected with urban area by expressway.

3.2.1 Analysis on the Status Quo of China's Tourism Industry Structure

Firstly, China's tourism product is single and the product portfolio has not taken shape. Many touristic areas in China mainly rely on sightseeing, and the development of destinations for vacation travel cannot satisfy the needs of tourists, and the development of a specific type of tourism destinations has not really started. The product structure in most old touristic areas is unreasonable, single and non-systematic. Therefore, the whole product portfolio is lacking in variety and diversity.

Secondly, the inadequacy of transport capacity for tourism has limited the formation of the tourism economy in scale. This is mainly due to the small size of planes, the backward construction of airports, the slow increase in international routes and flights, the serious overloading of passenger's trains, the lack of train lines departing from the cities considered as tourism hubs, the level of roads, the poor quality of roads, and other security problems in highways leading to touristic zones. The travel boats or ships too are still outdated in hardware configuration and slow in speed as well.

Thirdly, the tourist accommodation facilities are not corresponding with the pace of development of the tourism industry. The hotels are mainly located in the metropolis towns where competition is fierce. On the contrary, in many touristic attractions with a large number of travelers, especially in some central towns or cities with famous scenic spots, the number of star hotels is obviously limited, the four-star hotels and five-star hotels in particular are scarce. No hotel groups have been organized for these star hotels, not to mention chain operation, consequently, the hotel occupancy is low and anti-risk capacity is weak. As a result, these hotels are obviously awkward when competing with the foreign chain hotel groups in China. Worse of all is that the hotel industry lacks the ability to adjust its layout to the latest market conditions. Presently, the hotel industry only supplies the sightseeing-type hotel, with a series of other products waiting to be supplemented, such as business hotels, executive hotels, conference hotels, vacation hotels, vacation apartments, youth hostels and motels, etc.

Fourthly, the recreational facilities are not perfect, and the recreational items are monotonous. Due to the fact that the vacation tour and specific tour had just started in the China, some recreational facilities are still not in perfect shape, and the recreational items are monotonous. The recreational product which is suitable for family and children is too few in scenic spots, so there is still a long way to go for the tapping of recreational activities with local features.

Fifthly, the taste of the tourism product is awful, so it occupies only a small proportion in the consumption ratio of tourists. The design, production, and sales of tourism products cannot satisfy the demands of the tourism market; the weakness in research and development capacity results in the lack of its attraction. There is also lack of theme, variety and series in tourism products. To a greater extent, the tourism products still cannot get rid of the subordinate position to foreign trade.

Sixthly, the catering industry is large in number, wide in domain and low in quality and its products are lacking in characteristics and cultural flavor, which result in the weak competition of the catering industry.

Seventhly, the tourism industry is not outstanding as a leading industry, and also it does not produce enough economic benefits. Presently, in terms of layout, the travel agency industry can be described as "small, scattered, weak and poor", therefore the industry obviously lacks the competitiveness to fight against risks from the market. Concerning the organizational system, instead of dividing travel agencies into wholesalers and the retailers based on the international conventions and the market principle, they were divided into international and domestic travel agencies based on business scope. Therefore, China's travel agencies own low capacity to explore the tourism market, especially the international tourism market. It also lacks the ability to build a huge distribution network system at home and aboard.

3.2.2 Adjusting Direction of China's Tourism Industry Structure at Present

The whole tourism industry is presently at the adjustment stage, combining the development of vacation tourism with the development of life experience as the center. The details are as follows: (1) to deepen and improve tourism products and build a multiple industrial structure by accelerating the development of different types of products to meet different demands; (2) to adjust the industrial integration by sparing no efforts to promote integration and achieve general development, comprehensive development, scale development and multi-industrialization; (3) to adjust the industrialization of tourism destinations by strengthening the integration of tourism destinations, encouraging regional optimization, characteristic development and town travel, so as to form the two-way trend of industrial destination and destination industrialization; (4) to start formulating laws and regulations for vacation system, vacation product, tourism capital goods and the exploitation of tourism product market; and (5) to explore new concepts of life experiences and life style by following the humanistic approaches and promoting change of life style.

3.3 Analysis of China's Tourism Product Structure

3.3.1 Formation and Types of Tourism Product

After over 40 years of China's reform and opening up, the tourism industry in China has formed a scale of production. The characteristics of tourism product are shown as follows:

(1) The traditional tourism projects, such as sightseeing tour, vacation tour and visiting of relatives and friends have entered into a mature period and it has developed a scale of production that can meet the needs of tourists.
(2) The difference of market trend existing between inbound tourists and domestic tourists market concentrates on two types of products: the inbound tourists on business tour outnumber those visiting relatives and friends while the domestic tourists visiting relatives and friends on the contrary outnumber those on business tour.
(3) Newly-designed tourism products begin to emerge. Conference tour, sports tour, education tour, health tour and adventure tour are able to meet the needs of tourists of different age groups, income level and cultural background.

3.3.2 *Characteristics of China's Tourism Products*

Firstly, from the strengths of its tourism products, China is rich in cultural, social and natural attractions, which are the knockout products of its tourism industry. China enjoys more than five thousand years of civilizations and brilliant cultures, which has endowed the nation with many historical sites and heritages, such as the Forbidden City,[3] the Great Wall and Terra-Cotta Warriors[4] which are very famous in the world. The harmonious relationship among all the 56 nationalities in China has contributed to a rich and colorful folk style in China. China boasts of a vast territory and diverse climate, which helps the formation of peculiar natural landscapes in thousands of postures, such as Guilin's Landscape and the Three Gorges of the Yangtze River. With the economic development in recent years, inbound tourists are able to enjoy more convenience in sightseeing, catering, accommodation, transportation, shopping and entertainment. In addition, more and more inbound tourists coming to China feel at home because of China's stable political situation, sound public security and hospitality of the Chinese (Figs. 3.3 and 3.4).

Secondly, from tourism market advantages, many tourists are traveling to China from different countries every year. The 30 million overseas Chinese distributed around the world is an important stable source of tourists traveling back to China. The tourism market in neighboring countries is promising and with strong potential. This year, more than one million Japanese tourists are expected to visit China. The tourism markets of Korea, Malaysia and Indonesia have reached a certain scale and continue to grow at a relatively fast speed. And the number of tourists travelling to China from America and Europe has maintained a steady growth momentum. Moreover, various

[3]The Forbidden City, was the Chinese imperial palace from the Ming dynasty to the end of the Qing dynasty—the years 1420–1912. It is located in the center of Beijing, and now houses the Palace Museum.

[4]The Terra Cotta Warriors, as the accessory funeral objects of the First Emperor Qin (259-B.C.210), are regarded as one of the Great Miracles in the world and ranks the top attraction in China, together with the Great Wall.

Fig. 3.3 The Forbidden city

Fig. 3.4 The Terra-Cotta Warriors

kinds of special interest tourism, such as business tourism, individual tourism, etc., are growing rapidly.

3.3.3 *Analysis of Main Problems of China's Tourism Product Structure*

3.3.3.1 The External Problems of China's Tourism Product Structure

(1) Imbalanced in structure: the proportion of few tourism products is too high, especially the proportion of sightseeing;
(2) Low development level: most tourism resources still stay in surface development and are under the category of primary tourism products;
(3) Low market profits: the added value and extended value of tourism products are low and lacking in multiple profit structure;
(4) Low involvement in overseas market: for instance, the sightseeing of overseas cultural relics and historical sites is based on the vertical division of the international tourism market.

3.3.3.2 Thorough Exploration of China's Tourism Product Structure

(1) Several generations of products formed along with the industrial stage. The development of the first generation of tourism product highly relied on natural resources, and the core products were even equal to natural resources. The core product type of this generation mainly included the sightseeing product represented by well-known mountains and rivers, scenic spots and historic sites, which belong to the primary development of tourism products. The development of the second generation of tourism products is not entirely dependent on the distribution of the natural resources, instead it laid more emphasis on the market demand. With the segmentation of the tourism industry market, various specific products, which are non-sightseeing and non-public emerged, such as business tour, sports tour, adventure tour, convention tour, honeymoon tour and folk custom tour, etc. However, the design idea is not mature, there is no obvious breakthrough in the content arrangement of the product. Although the product form is diverse, the content is mostly the same. So far, China's tourism products still belong to the first and second generations, and the development of the third generation of tourism products has just begun to sprout up. With the advent of the era of experience economy, the core tourism products require more and more situational participation and interaction.
(2) Defects in the development mode of the primary tourism products. Although at the specific stage of development, it only takes only a short time to produce a quick effect in the development of primary tourism products, the development

relies strongly on natural resources and it is more like the "killing-hen-for-eggs" mode of development. Furthermore, the development mode is highly restricted by the location of natural resources and lacks connectivity with the market.

(3) Consequence of the dominant position of sightseeing. This situation is not only in contradiction with the trend of domestic market supply and demand but also goes against the horizontal division of labor of China's tourism market in the international market, thus leading to a very low market share of China's tourism products in the huge global non-sightseeing tourism market.

(4) Improvement in economy and culture brought a change in psychological need. With the improvement of people's living conditions, the DIY (Do-it-Yourself) tour and self-drive tour have become a trend and Under this background, it is necessary to perfect the tourism products by making them individualized, thematic and special.

(5) Life circle of tourism products. A tourism destination may not necessarily have a life circle but a tourism product does have. A tourism destination is merely the carrier of tourism products, and different tourism products can be derived from the same tourism destination after having been improved and promoted. The life circle of tourism products requires timely adjustment of product structure and level according to the market trend.

(6) Change in the traffic conditions. Traditional sightseeing to a certain extent results from backward transportation, whereas non-sightseeing tourism, such as vacation travel, demands faster and more comfortable transportation. Presently, the improvement of the traffic conditions has provided a basis for the updating of tourism products.

(7) Change in social ideology. The change of social concepts has resulted in new hot tourism spots. For example, the growing awareness of ecological protection in the whole world leads to the popularity of eco-tourism products.

(8) The unbalanced development of tourism products as a result of the basic national condition. Tourism products are subject to the stage of tourism development, and the tourism industry is subject to the level of economic development. Concerning tourism development in China, the basic situation is that: tourism is highly developed along the coastal regions in the east and southeast, but less developed in central China and least developed in the west of the country. This basic situation also requires that from the whole nation, the form of tourism products must be diversified.

(9) The internal relation between product development and market order. The low level and monotonous type of tourism products lead to the maladjustment of the market order. For example, the same tourism route is usually run by many different travel agencies, which of course will result in vicious competition, such as price reduction, etc.

(10) **Inner link among product, market and profit**. Different tourism products target different tourism markets while different tourism markets certainly differ in profit making. Generally, revenue of the sightseeing product is low while revenue of the vacation tour, business tour and convention tour is high, which

has been proved by the practice of foreign tourism in the course of development. China's tourism products lack qualities of amusement and tourists' participation, which leads to a restriction in profit making. Therefore, China's tourism revenue is relatively low when compared with some other countries in the world.

3.3.4 *Countermeasures for China's Tourism Product Structure Under the New Situation*

From the above analyses, it is clear that China's current tourism product structure is still in the primary stage of maturity, which is reflected in the formation of a certain product structure system. The primary sightseeing product has been mature, the speed of tourist growth tends to be steady and the tourism investment has produced good economic and social benefits. The features of the core tourism products of the main scenic spots are distinguishing but their attraction to the return tourists is decreasing gradually. However, the influx of large number of first-time tourists has imposed severe challenges on the social and environmental loading capacity of tourism destinations. Therefore, it is a must to improve the tourism product structure as a result of the market competition and the emergence of new tourism products; otherwise, China's tourism products will fall into the stage of recession.

(1) To optimize sightseeing products. Optimizing sightseeing products entails optimizing the traditional sightseeing products which have been developed into state-level sightseeing products in the second generation represented by seven major touristic cities. It mainly relies on the "soft treatment", including the innovation of sightseeing forms and performance. The so-called second generation of state-level sightseeing products refers to the new touristic attractions with huge potential and nationwide significance, which have entered into the overseas tourism markets, such as the Silk Road,[5] the Three Parallel Rivers, the Mt. Huang,[6] the Yangzi River and Tibet, etc. (Figs. 3.5 and 3.6)
(2) Business tour. With the further internationalization of the world economy and the development of China's export-oriented economy, business tour had risen despite that it was not highly developed. With the further development of the market economy, tourism departments especially the domestic travel agencies should actively work with economic and trade departments concerned to bring out business tours.

---

[5]The Silk Road or Silk Route, is an ancient network of trade and cultural transmission routes that were central to cultural interaction through regions of the Asian continent connecting the West and East by merchants, pilgrims, monks, soldiers, nomads, and urban dwellers from China and India to the Mediterranean Sea during various periods of time.

[6]Mt. Huang, located in the south of Anhui province in central China, it is probably the most famous mountain and one of the great symbols of the country.

Fig. 3.5 The Silk Road

Fig. 3.6 The Mt. Huang

(3) Domestic official tour. The official tour here refers to the tour type where matters, such as transportation, accommodation, catering and conferences in official affairs are arranged by travel agencies abiding by the international conventions. An official tour organized by travel agencies has such advantages: firstly, the price offered by travel agencies is usually less expressive than that of self-organized tours; therefore, it can help organizations concerned to reduce administrative and business cost; secondly, it can bring convenience to its clients;

thirdly, it is helpful to regulate official tours in terms of finance. The official tour in China is a new concept and is only being tried in few big cities, such as Shanghai.

(4) International convention tour. The international convention tourism in China is undeveloped. The international convention tour market is specialized and characterized by sharp expansion and high-consumption. China is able to develop such a market actively and specifically all by itself because: it has the established open-door policies, adequate accommodation facilities for such conventions, and it also possesses the world-class sightseeing resources. Unfortunately for the time being, China not only lacks the sales promotion but also lacks macro promotion and coordination in this domain, which requires departments at all levels to deepen their understanding and enhance promotion of the product.

(5) Medical and health tour. In overseas, the traditional market has profound relations with the aging population in the developed countries. Currently China has just stepped into the time of aging, and it can be predicted that the future of medical and health tour in China will be promising referring to the international experience. Moreover, with the concept of natural medicine and natural therapies being expanded in many countries, China has its own unique traditional medicine, which is a huge advantage for her to vigorously develop this tourism product. Therefore, tourism departments should take the initiative to cooperate with pharmaceutical departments to actively develop this product (Fig. 3.7).

(6) Specific tour. This type of tourism aims to satisfy people's special needs, including tasty food tour, adventure tour, folk-custom tour and study tour, etc. The market of such is narrow and stable but it brings in high profits. Expanding such a market mainly depends on the innovative consciousness and market awareness of travel agencies.

(7) Vacation tour. It is one of the main parts of overseas tourism markets, especially in the developed countries. The conditions for developing far-distance vacation tours in China are not as good as for sightseeing tours. On the one hand, only the beach vacation resource of Hainan province is unique and can rival with the international excellent beaches; therefore, Hainan needs to enhance the development of the tour. On the other hand, there are great potentials for the tapping of short-distance vacation tours, such as the rural home inns along the outskirts of cities. With the process of urbanization in China, this market is becoming bigger and bigger.

(8) Ice-snow sports tour. The winter sports tour owns a big market and especially has a huge positive effect on making use of tourism markets in slack seasons. China has a vast territory where the cold areas in the North have the resources for developing the tour since people in the warm areas have such a travel demand. The development of the product is of great benefit for balancing seasonality of product development and promoting interaction among tourism-generating regions.

(9) Compound tourism products. This type of tour can help to satisfy tourists' composite demands. Nowadays, tourists' tourism demands have increasingly become varied and compound and the number of tourists with only a single

Fig. 3.7 Traditional Chinese medicine

purpose in traveling is decreasing day by day. To adapt to this trend, it is necessary to vigorously develop a two-in-one and all-in-one tourism products, such as business plus sightseeing, sightseeing plus vacation, convention plus sightseeing, and study plus sightseeing, etc. This task is mainly undertaken by travel agencies.

3.4 Diversity of China's Tourism Product

3.4.1 From Sightseeing Tour to the Primary Development of China's Tourism Products

At the initial stage of tourism development in China, the main part of tourism products was the sightseeing product. Nearly 70% of tourists traveling in China before 1987 were travelling for the purpose of sightseeing, and its proportion reduced gradually by 1990. However the sightseeing tour still currently ranks first.

From 1979 to the 1990s, China put forward the policy of "striving to develop tourism industry" and the national tourism authority began to consciously develop compound tourism products. The product development mainly depends on the major touristic cities and tourism routes, while putting the main objective on the international tourism market.

Sightseeing is one of the most basic parts of tourism activities and it had also been one of the most basic activities since the ancient times. From the perspective of the tourism economy, the sightseeing product is the most direct use of tourism resources. Any place can be open to tourists as long as it is equipped with natural or humanistic resources appealing to tourists, and basic necessary traffic conditions. With respect to other forms of tourism, sightseeing has a low demand for the developed degree of social economy and service level of the tourism industry, and in a certain sense, it is an easier way of making use of tourism resources. Therefore, sightseeing has become the leading product in the tourism industry and the major driving force for tourism development in China.

Modern marketing theory holds that any product has its life circle, that is, any product in the market has to go through the process of production, growth, maturity and decline. However, the tourism product of sightseeing is not a tangible product, therefore, it does not have a typical life circle like tangible products. To overcome the negative effects on tourism development brought about by limitations of sightseeing, it is of great necessity to develop new types of tourism products.

3.4.2 *Diversity of China's Tourism Product*

Starting from the beginning of 1990s, the national tourism authority and tourism business circle have paid attention to exploit China's tourism resources which are rich and colorful to develop various types of tourism products. From 1992, the CNTA has been setting different tourism themes every year to lay particular emphasis on promoting the country's tourism products. The activity's themes from 1992 to 2017 are:

1992—Visit China Tour
1993—China Landscape Tour
1994—China Heritage Tour
1995—China Folklore Tour
1996—China Resort Tour
1997—Travel-in-China Tour
1998—China Urban & Rural Tour
1999—China Eco-Environment Tour
2000—China New Millennium Tour
2001—China Sports & Fitness Tour
2002—China Folk Arts Tour
2003—China Culinary Tour
2004—China Catch the Lifestyle Tour
2005—Travel in China Year

2006—China Rural Tour
2007—China Harmonious Urban and Rural Tour
2008—China Olympics Tourism Year
2009—China Ecological Tourism Year
2010—China World Expo Tourism Year
2011—China Culture Tourism Year
2012—China Happiness & Health Tour
2013—China Marine Tourism Year
2014—Beautiful China: Year of Smart Travel
2015—Beautiful China, Year of Silk Road Tourism
2016—Beautiful China, Year of Silk Road Tourism
2017—Beautiful China, Year of Silk Road Tourism (Figs. 3.8 and 3.9).

The special theme activities organized by the CNTA are deepening, unfolding and improving step by step, and its efforts are highly appreciated by the international tourism industry, and the activities are considered as the gradual maturity of China's tourism industry and its integration into the global tourism family. The national special promotions have improved the overall image of China's tourism industry, it had highlighted the features of China tourism resources and tourist service products and had played a big role in promoting China's inbound tourism.

With more than 40 years of development in its tourism industry, China's tourism product has formed a tripod pattern of sightseeing, vacation and specific tourism products. The specific tour most especially has witnessed powerful momentum in development in recent years, which mainly covers industrial tourism, agricultural tourism, eco-tourism and festival and exhibition tourism, etc.

Fig. 3.8 Beijing Olympic Games 2008

Fig. 3.9 Shanghai World Expo 2010

Industrial tourism refers to the tourism activities which has as aim to familiarize tourists with the production process and relevant products of the industrial enterprises concerned and tourists equally can get chances to learn about some information about production, performance and quality of the industrial products introduced, so as to deepen their understanding of the consumer goods. Enterprises carrying out industrial tourism take it as a good channel to communicate with the visiting tourists, advertise their products and show the features of their products and the proficiency of production, so as to strengthen the interaction with tourists, establish the enterprise image, cultivate and expand the market.

Domestic industrial tourism emerged in the 1990s and the enterprises involved are some famous enterprises such as Haier Group, Qingdao Beer Group, Nongfu Spring Company, Nanjing Iron & Steel Co. Ltd, Dongfeng Peugeot Citroen Automobile Company Ltd and Linuo Group, etc. Nowadays more and more well-known industrial enterprises in China welcome tourists to visit them in an appropriate way. The industrial tourism is being carried out in some few fields, and the industrial projects involved ranging from the manufacturing process of automobile, steel, industrial wharf, wine making, beverage, appliance, cement, to petroleum and food, etc.

Because the urbanization progress is quickening and people had started yearning for the pure rural life, rural tourism began to thrive. Although the concept of rural tourism is not united and the product forms may be diverse such as rural inns, folk performance and participation in rural labor, their common feature is that the touristic source for rural tourism comes from cities where tourists leave their city life to receive the tourism experience through visiting or participating in the rural life and labor work.

Eco-tourism[7] is an emerging tourism product which appeared under the influence of the sustainable development concept. Since the 1990s, China has successively promoted a series of eco-tourism products and has attracted a batch of tourists interested in the specific natural or cultural environment. A large number of touristic attractions began to consider eco-tourism as their future selling point and many state reserves mainly focused on carrying out eco-tourism. The launch of the eco-tourism activities helped to promote the construction of relevant ecological touristic attractions. A typical example is the construction of China's Shangri-la ecological tourism zone, presently it is the biggest highland ecological touristic zone in the world. It was jointly invested by the Sichuan province, Yunan province and The Tibet autonomous region with an amount ranging from 50 to 80 billion RMB (Fig. 3.10).

The festival and exhibition tourism is being developed by leaps and bounds in China and has become one of the most important tourism forms. Due to the fact that conferences, incentive travel and exhibition have basically similar features, such a market is internationally named as MICE (the shortened form of Meeting, Incentives, Conferences and Exhibition). According to the statistics recorded by the International Congress and Convention Association (ICCA) in the 1990s, each year more than 400,000 of various international conferences are held and are attended by over 50 international participants from four or more countries, with the total conference expenditure surpassing 280 billion US dollar. Originally, conferences and exhibitions in China were organized by the government and they were rarely linked to tourism mainly for certain political or economic purposes. With the economic development, people began to realize the importance of MICE, which not only have an

Fig. 3.10 Shangri-la ecological tourism zone

[7]Eco-tourism, is a form of tourism involving visiting fragile, pristine, and relatively undisturbed natural areas, intended as a low-impact and often small scale alternative to standard commercial (mass) tourism. Its purpose may be to educate the traveler, to provide funds for ecological conservation, to directly benefit the economic development and political empowerment of local communities, or to foster respect for different cultures and for human rights.

effect on attracting merchants and promoting local image but can also bring in good economic benefits. For this reason, many regions all over the country are competing to hold regional, national and even international conferences. According to relevant researches, the number of conferences of various kinds increases progressively with a speed of about 20% annually in our country since the 1980s. Now, MICE-related activities are involved in all respects and fields in the society such as in politics, economy, culture, technology, education, hygiene and military, among which most of them are focuses of concern for people from all walks of life in their daily social lives, Therefore, they are of great significance for the promotion of tourism development. The organization of some large-scale activities such as the Olympics and World Expo most especially, has a profound and long lasting impact on tourism. For example, through the hosting of the World Horticulture Expo in 1999, Kunming received 549,000 overseas tourists and harvested tourism receipts of about 145 million US dollars in the same year. An increase of 44.5% against 43.6% of the previous year was recorded. Kunming received 11.5 million domestic tourists and earned a total revenue of 10.4 billion RMB, an increase of 23.3% against 48.6% of the year 1998 (Fig. 3.11).

With the improvement of China's economic and social development and international influence, the MICE-related activities held in China predicted a rapid growth. The 2008 Beijing Olympic Games and the 2010 Shanghai World Expo have been the new drive for the promotion of tourism development in China. According to the

Fig. 3.11 Kunming World Horticulture Expo

data statistics by the official website of Shanghai World Expo, the World Expo had attracted 70 million tourists to Shanghai. No matter the aspect from which it can be perceived, the conference and exhibition industry has huge potential for future development both in China and the outside world and it is also one of the hottest industries with the most promising and biggest potential for development in the twenty-first century. The MICE-related tourism became a powerful driving force for the development of China's tourism.

Currently, China's tourism products are very rich in form and content, including both the form and the content of the tourism activities and the tourism means. Simply speaking, China has basically developed a product system which considers the sightseeing tour, vacation tour and specific tour as the three major subjects. In the course of diversifying its tourism products, the most important problem faced by China is how to use its human resources to develop diversified products, given that China is a very large country that possesses much human resources.

For the convenience of tourists, while paying attention to the development of the modern social culture, it is of great necessity for China to establish many man-made landscapes so as to enable the materialization of intangible resources based on the protection and utilization of existing historical human landscapes. It is also necessary to renovate, imitate and create a batch of human landscapes for tourists to visit and engage in cultural and recreational activities. Through these efforts, the expected result is to integrate man-made landscapes with existing historical landscapes so as to create a complete landscape system. This will reveal the cultural connotation of the system from different angles and levels.

The development tendency of modern tourism products is based on increasing tourists' participation in the product, therefore tourists are expected to get enjoyment and satisfaction in the process of participation. As long as a product can catch up with the development trend of the era, it can have effect on attracting tourists. However from the reality of the world tourism development, it is a general trend to improve the participation and amusement of tourism activities. Therefore, the fact that people can never overlook is that they should plan and construct proper human landscapes, design appropriate tourist projects with tourists' strong participation and combine human landscapes with sightseeing, vacation, cultural communication and amusement so as to make tourists better understand the practice of tourism reception.

Reference

Song Z (2006) Research on China contemporary tourism development. Economic Management Press, Beijing

Chapter 4
System Changes in China's Tourism Development

China's tourism industry had experienced or is still undergoing three stages in the economy transition. The first stage involves the striving for more foreign exchange, the second stage involves the stimulation of domestic demand and the third stage involves the stimulation of economic growth. Throughout the three stages, the government serves as the subject, that is to say, the government establishes the objective of tourism development according to the current situation of the macro economy. The government also selects other organizations and groups and gives them the possibility to be involved in the whole process by means of institutional arrangement (guideline or policy).

4.1 Evolution of China's Tourism Management System Since the Reform and Opening-Up

4.1.1 To Improve the Tourism Management System

Tourism management system refers to two political and economic structures which are inter-connected and are also distinct from one another. These systems are: the system of administrative control and the economic management system. The former has as duty to realize daily leading, supervision and provide necessary support for tourism at all levels of national administrative departments that are involved. The latter means that professional tourism enterprises in operation carry out economic management in each department within the enterprise, outside the enterprise and in each type of enterprise, that is, the tourism enterprise and the non-tourism enterprise for healthy development based on the objective law of the economy. For China's tourism development, the national macro tourism management system plays a decisive role, therefore, its characteristics should be the focus for research, including the administrative organizations and their duties, the tourism management regulations

© Social Sciences Academic Press and Springer Nature Singapore Pte Ltd. 2019

P. Zhou, *The Theory and Practice of China's Tourism Economy (1978–2017)*,
Research Series on the Chinese Dream and China's Development Path,
https://doi.org/10.1007/978-981-32-9107-2_4

and forms, etc. The organizational system for tourism management is the basis for operation in the whole tourism management system. Presently, almost all countries have established special organizations to manage affairs relating to tourism.

4.1.1.1 China Has Established a Set of Relatively Complete Institutional Systems for Tourism Management in the Course of Tourism Development

From the hierarchical perspective, tourism management organizations are divided into central authority and local authority. From the functional perspective, it can be divided into administrative organizations and industrial organizations. The national tourism management organizations are mainly the National Tourism Committee and the China National Tourism Administration (CNTA). The National Tourism Committee manages the daily affairs of tourism and coordinates the organizations established by the State Council, and all the department heads of the State Council are members of the Committee. The Committee is mainly responsible for discussing important policies and guidelines, development policies and the major projects concerning national tourism development. The committee also coordinates or solves the problems which its subordinate departments or local tourism authorities are unable to solve. The CNTA is the department in charge of tourism directly under the State Council and exercises tourism management functions entirely.

4.1.1.2 Consistent Improvement of Tourism Industry Organizations

By the end of 2012, China had about a dozen of national industry associations, namely: China Tourism Association, China Women Tourism Committee (subordinate to China Tourism Association), China Touristic Cities Association (subordinate to China Tourism Association), China Association of Travel Services, China Touristic Hotels Association, China Tourism Automobile and Cruise Association and China Association of Tourism Journals etc. Among them, the China Tourism Association is found inside the China National Tourism Administration (CNTA), its heads are officials from China National Tourism Administration, and the Association carries out its main duty by working in conjunction with the CNTA and has 146 affiliated members.

It is necessary to point out that the tourism associations in China rely heavily on the government or are controlled by the government. They cannot provide adequate genuine enterprise services such as the decision on the industrial disputes, the formulation of industrial standards, timely release of information, specification of the trade rules and safeguard of member interests. Therefore industrial interests cannot be soundly protected by these associations. However, in the countries where the market economy is more developed, industry associations are non-governmental organizations organized form bottom to top and their primary task is to serve and help members to enhance common interests and promote industry development. The healthy development of China's tourism also calls for the due functions played by the industry association. They should be able to improve the quality of industry associations and should also shoulder the responsibility of industrial communication, management and service.

4.1.2 Tourism Management System in the Period of Foreign Affairs Reception and Service

The tourism management system in China had not undergone fundamental changes before the year 2008, and its major problems can be summarized as follows:

(1) The management system was basically affiliated to foreign affairs, thus lacking due independence; (2) The tourism administration and tourism management were mixed up and there was no clear distinction between government administration and enterprises; (3) There no specific laws and regulations for tourism management and reception services, and the management and services were almost based on the laws and regulations and policy documents for the management of foreigners coming to China issued by the state. Fortunately, all these problems are gradually being solved.

4.1.3 Gradual Improvement of the Reform and Opening-Up Policy and Tourism Management System

Since 1978, the nature of China's tourism has had a fundamental change and the tourism management system in China has also experienced significant and profound reform. In March 1978, the reform on the tourism management organization was carried out. The China Travel Business Administration was renamed as the 'Tourism Bureau directly under the State Council', controlled by the Ministry of Foreign Affairs. Tourism administrative bureaus were established in all provinces, cities and regions responsible for tourism affairs. A leading group of tourism business was established and the leaders from the State Council were appointed as supervisor and deputy supervisor. The leaders from other ministries or committees—the planning commission, construction committee, foreign trade, light industry, commerce, railway, transportation and civil aviation, etc. were appointed as group members. The main responsibilities of the leading group were: To examine and approve of the policies and guidelines concerning tourism; examine the development planning and the construction planning of touristic areas for the nation's tourism industry; perform a balancing act in dealing with all the tourism-related affairs under its charge, examine tourism plans and inspect the implementation. Other specific affairs were in the charge of the CNTA.

4.2 Development of Government-Led Tourism System

4.2.1 Formation of Government-Led Tourism Development Theory

The development of government-oriented tourism requires giving full play to the leading role of the government to seek for better the development of tourism in accordance with its characteristics and with its market as the major allocation resource. China is now in the process of establishing market economy system, and its tourism development is mainly under the control of the government at all levels and the government plays a dominant part in tourism development, thus whether the achievements made or the problems arising have a lot to do with this phenomenon. In other words, the tourism development is government-oriented in China. The government-oriented development of tourism in China can be perceived from two aspects: In reality, the government has been the leading force in national economic development due to the current situation of China's economic system, and naturally the tourism development is government-oriented. In theory, the mode of government-oriented tourism development or the strategy for tourism development has been arrived at mainly by mirroring the experience of economic development in East Asia, Japan and other countries similar to China's practical situation.

4.2.2 Transformation of the Form and System of Government's Leading Role

Government's leading role in tourism embodies different connotations at different stages. China's tourism started in the context of planned economy in the late 1970s. The government's control over the tourism industry was inevitably invested with planned economy. At that time, the tourism industry had not gained the due industrial position to satisfy the needs of inbound tourists streaming into China due to reform and opening-up. Consequently, what the government needed to do urgently was to build touristic hotels, develop travel agencies and tap tourism resources, etc. At the macro level and micro level, the government mainly used direct management as a way to manage tourism, and tourism development depended mainly on governmental forces. As a matter of fact, government's leading role was a kind of direct control as a result of the lack of market economy foundation at the moment. From the perspective of the CNTA, its overall management shall be executed over tourism activities involving transportation, sightseeing, accommodation, catering, shopping and entertainment, etc.

Since the new millennium, great changes have also taken place in the form of the government's dominant role, that is, from direct intervention to indirect control mainly by economic means. From the perspective of management mode over tourism by the government, with the gradual improvement of the market economic system and the constant deepening of the reform on government institutions, the law-based control over tourism is now becoming the main mechanism of government-oriented tourism.

4.2.3 Effect Evaluation of Government-Led Tourism Development

China's tourism service had always been an auxiliary section for foreign affairs since the founding of the new China and it focused only on political needs other than economic benefits. After the 3rd Plenary Session of the 11th CPC Central Committee, [1] tourism started its transition in a tough way. 20 years later, the government's leading role became the main force in the rapid development of China's tourism, and it is safe to say that without government's leading role, there would have been no such rapid development in China's tourism. More so, the significance of government's leading role in tourism development is mainly presented in the following aspects (Fig. 4.1).

Firstly, the rapid development in the supply ability of tourism service has been realized. The principal contradiction of tourism development had been demand inflation versus supply shortage experienced till the end of "The Cultural Revolution" [2]in

Fig. 4.1 The 3rd Plenary session of the 11th CPC central committee

[1]The 3rd Plenary Session of the 11th CPC Central Committee, held in 1978, is a meeting of the most profound historical significance in China's modern history, marking the end of the social and ideological chaos after the Cultural Revolution and paving the way for China's opening-up and economic construction.

[2]The Cultural Revolution, was a social-political movement that lasted from 1966 until 1976, and the movement paralyzed China politically and significantly affected the country economically and socially.

1976. The solution to deal with the contradiction was to centralize forces in every aspect to vigorously construct tourism service facilities (Fig. 4.2).

Secondly, tourism's industrial position has been established. With the development of tourism economy, tourism's contribution to national economy and social development had become increasingly obvious. Bit by bit, China's tourism had won a place in the social economic development plan and tourism had gained a greater opportunity for development. Presently, tourism has been the new growth point in the national economy and the pillar industry in many areas.

Thirdly, both the domestic and the foreign markets grow steadily. Under the overall organization by the CNTA, China's domestic and international markets witnessed rapid growth, outbound tourism grew gradually and China had become the new largest emerging tourism-generating market in the world.

Fourthly, the management system had been improving constantly. China's tourism has developed over the past 20 years at an exceptional rate. Since various interest in the industry needed to be coordinated, the market order had to be maintained and the industrial structure had to be continuously adjusted, the industrial management system of tourism emerged and constantly improved in the process.

Relationships in all respects needed to be straightened out because China's economic system was still in the process of transition. Therefore, the government authorities of the tourism administration still needed to play an important and irreplaceable role in industrial management and undertook more important tasks than the governments of developed market economy. Undeniably, just like a coin which has two sides, the government-oriented mode has its inherent weaknesses. In the process of

Fig. 4.2 The cultural revolution

China's tourism development, problems of government-oriented mode were mainly manifested as follows.

4.2.3.1 Economic Benefit in the Industry Were Generally not High

Generally speaking, government departments are non-profit institutions. When the tourism industry is under the guidance of government behavior, it pays more attention to overall development of the industry other than making profits. If attention is only focused to the leading role of government behavior in tourism while proper control is not provided over government behavior, in some circumstances, relevant departments of the government are likely to utilize resources under their control to excessively input for achievements, which will then result in the contradictory phenomenon whereby the industry develops rapidly while the economic revenue of tourism enterprises doesn't increase.

4.2.3.2 Suppress the Enthusiasm and Creativity of Tourism Enterprises

Under the market economy, enterprises and tourists are market subjects. Only high production efficiency of tourism enterprises can better satisfy tourists' overall needs and also enable tourism to develop in a healthy and stable way. Concerning the ownership system, China's tourism enterprises can mainly be divided into the state-owned business and the non-state-owned business and if the government is involved in business operation, it may inevitably result in unequal competition between enterprises of different ownership systems and thus suppress the development of the non-state-owned business. Even when is state-owned business, the government's involvement also deprives enterprises of due autonomy in management, in which case, the enterprises will fail to carry out the market economy. As for the government's intervention in tourism development, the government has good intentions towards tourism development but the actual result is unsatisfactory, and the intervention may suppress the enthusiasm and creativity of enterprises to produce and operate. It could also greatly weaken enterprises' market competitiveness.

4.2.3.3 Local Interest Conflict Results in Disordered Development of Tourism

It is undoubtedly true that tourism can help to promote economic development. Therefore in the government-oriented economy, the government shall naturally take various effective measures to vigorously develop tourism. However, the interests of governments at all levels are not necessarily consistent in the process of economic and social development and there usually exist all kinds of conflicts. Interest conflicts are inevitable between the superior and subordinate government departments and even between government departments of the same level, which generally result in some adverse effects. For instance, after the release of the "Five Together" policy (mentioned in Chap. 2), some problems arose in its implementation, which was mainly manifested in the aspect that the macro management of tourism was out of control and the micro management was out of order. To be more specific, hotel construction in hot tourism cities grew faster, and hotel scale and hotel level were unreasonable and the proportion of high-end hotels was too high; Grade A and Grade B travel agencies were unreasonable in structure and many Grade B travel agencies were operated out of business limit and raced to bring the price down, which resulted in disorder of the tourism market. Concerning the problems existing in the tourism industry, the deeper cause could be traced from the management system, and the principal contradiction rooted in the conflict between the central and various local interest subjects. Furthermore, some people think that improper policies implemented by the government may be prone to cause market disorder. When compared with the merely unfair competition between enterprises, it is more difficult to deal with such disorder and chaos.

Government departments at all levels pursue their own interest and they inevitably take some improper government behaviors in order to maintain their own interest, leading to vicious competition, local protection, over utilization of resources, environmental disruption and other phenomena in the development process of tourism. Due to the negative effects of government behaviors that are increasingly significant in tourism development, some people have suggested that government involvement should stop. However, as to whether government-oriented tourism development strategy should be applied or not, it would be unthinkable if there is lack of government's effective management in the process of tourism development. Even if some people are against the strategy of government-oriented tourism development, they are opposed to proper intervention by the government in tourism development, and what really matters is how to play the government role while at the same time perfecting the market mechanism.

4.2.4 Regulate Government Behavior and Promote Tourism Development

According to the theory of modern market economy, the role of government in market economy is that it is responsible for providing "institutional environment" for the economy, this mainly includes providing the rule of law, the protection of property rights, the market order and infrastructure. However from actual understanding, the government's role in economy is a little bit complicated. Some people think that there are three different circumstances which can be considered as "the hand of inaction", "helping hand" and "grabbing hand". In practice, the government is substantially in a dilemma, if the government is just a hand of inaction, then the smaller, the better; if it is only a grabbing hand, it shall be restricted as much as possible; if it is only a helping hand, the more powerful, the better. However, if the government is the combination of the "three hands", it will be difficult to design the system. The main objective is to encourage its role as the helping hand while restricting its role as the grabbing hand at the same time. The question we are faced with is how to understand the government's role and properly regulate government behavior. Attention should be specially focused on to the following aspects:

(1) To properly understand the meaning of "government leading". Making sure not to understand it as "being dominated by the government", "being financially dominated by the government" or "being controlled by the government", since our goal is to establish the socialist market economy system with the market as the basis of resource allocation. Government's leading role in tourism development is mainly manifested in policy, lawmaking and macro management of tourism, while we can neither count on the government to immediately participate in business activities of tourism enterprises nor frequently ask the government to increase investment in tourism.
(2) Globally speaking, direct governmental intervention in tourism tends to decrease. In the field of tourism management, apart from protecting and properly developing national museums and other historical buildings and providing tourism infrastructure, government intervention is characterized by retreating from all operations of tourism projects by the government.
(3) To guide social funds so as to increase investments in tourism according to the plan for tourism development. Governments at all levels should avoid direct investment as much as possible but should rather attract social capital entering into tourism by making preferential policies and measures. By doing so, the government can at the same time help enterprises to meet the capital need for tourism development and make the government itself stay out of the interest relationship, thus keeping government behavior impartial.
(4) To play a role in tourism promotion. Playing a role in tourism promotion by the government is also one of the points to be noted. With regards to the macro management of national tourism development, it is not possible for private sectors to bear all the heavy responsibilities in the national inbound tourism promotion on account of the particularity of tourism products. The proper practice is likely to be the so-called "joint state-private ownership" and its crucial point lies in the fact that government departments shall play the leading role in tourism promotion, including capital input.
(5) To play a leading role in the construction of tourism infrastructure and tourism environment. Tourism is a kind of comprehensive activity of strong dependency and its influence also involves every aspect of the social life. Infrastructure necessary for tourism activities is mostly strongly dependent which calls for strong support from the society in all respects. To be more concrete, it requires the government to broadcast the great significance of tourism activities to national economy and social development in a proper way and make proper arrangements for labor time for its citizens and social welfare, so as to create favorable conditions for tourism development. More so, someone proposed to make a national travel plan so as to turn traveling into people's indispensable common

consuming behavior and one of the basic national elements of life, and this proposition can have a far-reaching influence on China's tourism development if such measures can be implemented.

(6) To do intensify environmental protection and curb environmental pollution so as to ensure sustainable development of tourism. Tourism development relies on beautiful natural environment and favorable social environment. However, tourism development also brings in a lot of pressure on the natural environment and social environment and causes damage and pollution. This however helps to retard tourism development. In the process of tourism management, what most enterprises pursue are mere profits and they do not really care about environmental issues. Only the government is able to play the role by taking effective measures to prevent tourism activities from causing negative influence on natural and social environment and let tourism develop in a sustainable and healthy way.

References

Kuang L (2001) Study on development strategy of government-oriented tourism. China Travel & Tourism Press, Beijing

Song Z (2006) Research on China contemporary tourism development. Economic Management Press, Beijing

Sun S (1992) Face the choice of the 21st century: China tourism development strategy. People's Publishing House, Beijing

Wang D, Wei X Newly edited tourism economics. Shanghai People's Publishing House, Shanghai

Wei X, Liu Z, Zhang S (1999) Development trend of China's Tourism in the new century. Guangdong Tourism Press, Guangzhou

Zhang L (2002) Tourism administration. Higher Education Press, Beijing

Chapter 5
Tourism Development Modes and Development Experience with Chinese Characteristics

Through three decades of quick development after the reform and opening-up, China's tourism industry has basically gone through the development and growth periods, during which the government-oriented tourism industry development mode played a positive role. With the gradual complicated external environment of the tourism industry and constant increase of problems in the internal industry due to the continuously rapid growth, China's tourism has fallen into a contradiction of rapid growth and weak competitiveness. This implies that it has a big scale but poor a development quality, due to the fact that the government-oriented tourism development mode also has negative effects even though it mainly plays a positive role. However, China's tourism has formed some development modes reflecting its own characteristics during the 40 years of development, but the choice and innovation of the tourism development mode based on historical experience became a problem during this era when faced with rapid tourism development and fierce competition from the international market.

5.1 History of China's Tourism Development

After the Second World War, the emergence of the world tourism promoted the rapid development of the international trade service, which had become one of the biggest export items in the trade service. Due to the fact that tourism is a labor intensive industry based on resources, it is thus an industry characterized by small investments, fast effects and easy access compared with other industries. However, different countries use different ways to develop tourism.

Generally speaking, domestic tourism is the basis in the relationship between domestic and international tourism. The development of domestic tourism lays the foundation for resource exploitation, facilities construction and talent cultivation. International tourism is the extension and expansion of domestic tourism development, the natural product of the social and economic development and the natural

© Social Sciences Academic Press and Springer Nature Singapore Pte Ltd. 2019

P. Zhou, *The Theory and Practice of China's Tourism Economy (1978–2017)*,
Research Series on the Chinese Dream and China's Development Path,
https://doi.org/10.1007/978-981-32-9107-2_5

result of the economic development process. This is the general way of tourism development which conforms to the rules of the economic development, it gradually builds the tourism facilities in turns and accumulates the development experiences of the tourism economy, thus making tourism to develop in a healthy and orderly manner with a little negative effect. Therefore this pattern is generally adopted by most countries (including some developing countries).

China, as the biggest developing country, had explored a road different from that of most developed countries. Since the reform and opening-up, China considered solving the meager foreign exchange reserve as the starting point and wedged inbound tourism into the national economic system. This objectively had become an important component of national strategy. China's tourism has recovered and developed very fast, and has reached the assumed original purpose but it however gave birth to some problems. After entering into the 1990s, domestic tourism started rising and growing by leaps and bounds; outbound tourism has been in an ascending position in recent years. Therefore, China has realized the transformation from a big country with rich tourism resources to a tourism power in Asia, and is gradually fulfilling the historical goal of being a world tourism power.

5.2 China's Tourism Development Mode

5.2.1 Connotation of the Tourism Development Mode

How to choose a correct development mode for tourism development in every country is an important question that cannot be neglected. The so-called tourism development mode means a kind of tourism development way under which certain historical conditions and a series of ways, methods as well as roads are selected and executed by a country or region to realize its tourism development goals. It is a complete system, which consists of relevant elements such as concept, subject, object and tools, etc.

5.2.2 Different Modes of World Tourism Development

5.2.2.1 Division According to the Evolution Pattern of Tourism Development

The development modes of world tourism can be divided into two types according to the evolution mode of tourism growth. One is the extensive tourism economy development mode, namely the general development mode by which domestic tourism extends to the international tourism. The other is the propulsive tourism economy development mode, namely an unconventional development mode by which international tourism advances towards domestic tourism.

The so-called extended tourism economy development mode is a development mode under which the domestic tourism is first developed, then the inbound tourism and the outbound tourism through the development of the domestic tourism and finally realizes the all-round development of domestic tourism, inbound tourism and outbound tourism. The mode changed with the improvement of the productivity level and people's lifestyle. However, it turn tourism consumption into an important part of the people' life. Initially, people's tourism activities were limited within the boundary of their own country. With the increasingly strengthened demand for tourism, the domestic territory was unable to meet people's needs for tourism. Consequently, people started to go aboard, pushing the tourism development to extend from inbound to outbound.

5.2.2.2 Division from the Relationship Between the Formation and Development of Tourism and National Economy

From the relationship between the formation and development of tourism and national economy, tourism development mode can be divided into: the balanced mode and the unbalanced mode. The balanced tourism maintains a balanced developing speed, which is consistent with the overall developmental speed of the national economy. The tourism developing speed mentioned here refers to the overall speed of the whole tourism industry, which is not necessarily a consistent annual speed. If the whole developing speed of the tourism industry is consistent with that of national economy during a given period, it is called balanced-type pattern, while the unbalanced-type pattern means that tourism developing speed of a region is faster or slower than the whole developing speed of the national economy owing to the special policies and measures taken. Furthermore, the unbalanced type can be divided into the advanced type and the retarded type.

The advanced-type tourism development mode refers to a certain stage in which the formation and development of the tourism industry exceeds the whole development speed of the national economy, thus, the developing tourism drives and promotes the development of other industries related to the national economy and therefore leads to the booming of the economy in the whole region. This pattern generally happens in developing areas, where tourism resources are used to develop inbound tourism first with the support of the government to receive more foreign exchange needed for economic development, and then promotes the development of tourism under the support of the prosperous regional economy. The retarded-mode of tourism development suggests that when the national economy has developed to a certain stage, its tourism will naturally emerge and grow. With the economic development and the increase in people's income, people's tourism demand starts to produce and the society also develop the conditions to satisfy this need. This mode mainly occurs in developed areas.

5.2.2.3 Division from the Adjustment System of Tourism Development

When dividing from the adjustment system of the tourism development, tourism development can be divided into market-oriented development mode and government-oriented development mode. The market-oriented tourism development mode means that the development of the tourism economy considers the market mechanism as the core and realizes the optimal configuration of tourism through market regulation, which mainly relies on the market mechanism to adjust and realize the internal self-regulation and self-balance of tourism through the market. The market mechanism mainly consists of price mechanism, supply and demand mechanism and competitive mechanism. In this mode, the government mainly plays an indirect role in the macro control of the tourism development through the national industrial policies.

The government-oriented tourism development mode means that the government formulates tourism development programs or policies at each stage to realize its development. The characteristic of this pattern is that the government plays a leading role in the development of the tourism economy, including concept-guidance, policy-guidance, management-guidance and fund-guidance. In this pattern, the market mechanism still plays its role but it is mainly the role of assistance when compared to the macro control of the government.

5.2.2.4 Division from Difference Between Social Politics and Economic System

During the process of the development of the tourism industry in each country in the world, various kinds of development modes were shaped due to the differences in the social and political systems, degree of economic development, historical and cultural traditions, geographical position, the size of territory, customs, regional conditions and tourism resources, etc. The various modes represent the choices made by various countries based on their own local conditions, while avoiding their weaknesses and giving full play to their own advantages. This is also a comprehensive reflection of the basic conditions and strategies for tourism development in these countries. A suitable development mode also lays a foundation for the successful development of a country's tourism.

The former Soviet pattern refers to the traditional socialist pattern represented by the former Soviet Union and other countries like former Czechoslovakia, Poland, Romania and Hungary. Its characteristics were as follows: the domestic tourism served as a social welfare and their international tourism development started a little bit late and it was highly underdeveloped; the tourism industry was controlled by the tourism management organization of the government. However, this pattern gradually changed in the late 1990s, as it gradually transformed their tourism industry from the system of state-owned to that of private-owned, joint-stock and cooperative.

The former Yugoslavia pattern, represented by former Yugoslavia shows that the former Yugoslavia had made the earliest contact with Western countries and chose an open socialist path which is different from other socialist countries. Its characteristics were as follows: it carried out full opening-up with little state intervention, the enterprises had sufficient autonomy and governments took various measures to promote the rapid development of tourism in a macro view.

The American pattern refers to the countries that have a developed economy and a developed tourism. It is adopted by countries like America, Canada, Germany, Belgium, Netherlands, Norway and Japan. Its characteristics are as follows: the developed degree of tourism is synchronous with that of the national economy; tourism administration from government is relatively relaxed and indirect; tourism is mainly run by large enterprises, and most tourism enterprises are private; in terms of the development goal, gaining more foreign exchange is not the main goal for tourism development and the focus for tourism development changes with the actual situation of each individual country.

The Spain pattern, represented by Spain, refers to the pattern for the countries which share boundaries with the main tourism-generating countries, countries which have a good geographical location, and countries whose tourism resources are rich and unique and whose tourism industries are developed. Its characteristics are as follows: the countries concerned vigorously support the tourism industry and make it one of the pillar industries of their national economy; their tourism continues to develop in a high speed and the balance of payment in the international tourism is in surplus; it considers its neighboring countries as target markets and reduces tourism restrictions on them.

The Israel and Turkey pattern is the government-controlled pattern with Israel and Turkey as the typical examples. Its characteristics are: the countries concerned are organically combined with the market; order, prosperous and fast tourism growth is achieved through the compulsory intervention and the exercise of administrative power by the central government.

The India pattern, represented by India, refers to certain developing countries which are relatively backward in economy, and consider agriculture as the subject for national economy and are less developed in industry and commercial services. Its characteristics are: the countries concerned generally adopt the policy of advancing the development of international tourism while paying attention to the synchronous development of domestic tourism; in terms of tourism development, they adopt the mixed development system to develop state-owned enterprises and private enterprises simultaneously.

5.2.3 *Characteristics of Tourism Development Modes*

According to the basic concepts of philosophy, objects of the same kind have some main characteristics and similarities, the tourism development modes are no exception. Tourism development modes for each individual country share the following four common characteristics.

5.2.3.1 Guidance

The tourism development mode as the overall guideline for tourism development, is the essence of tourism development strategies. The tourism development mode generalizes the total concepts and basic features of tourism development strategies in a certain period and makes clear the inner requirement and development direction for tourism development strategies.

5.2.3.2 Development Stage

Tourism development modes have its time-validity and successful modes cannot do without the soil breeding its success—the political, economic and cultural environment. Different countries may adopt different tourism development modes according to their various national conditions in the various historical developmental periods.

5.2.3.3 Relative Stability

The tourism development mode not only has stage features but also has the feature of relative stability. The tourism development mode reflects the inherent regularity. As long as there is no qualitative change with the inner conditions and external environment for tourism development, the development mode should be kept relatively stable.

5.2.3.4 Specificity

During a certain period, the tourism development mode may be different from country to country due to the different degrees of tourism development. The successful development mode for the countries with developed tourism may not fit the countries whose tourism has just got started.

5.3 Tourism Development Modes with Chinese Characteristics

5.3.1 Traditional Tourism Development Modes

The research on the tourism development modes in China starts from the early 1980s. Chinese people's knowledge about the tourism development has experienced four stages in the past 20 years, which suggests that the tourism development mode is continuously developing and maturing in China.

5.3.1.1 Resource-Oriented Tourism Development Mode

Tourism resource is a generic term referring to various kinds of natural or humanistic objects which can attract people' motivation for tourism and be used to carry out tourism activities. Tourism resources serve as the foundation for tourism development. Attraction to tourists is the practical value and basic nature of tourism resources and also the important basis to distinguish whether an object belongs to tourism resource or not.

Generally speaking, the basic concept for regional tourism development in the 1980s considered regional analysis as the starting point. The various factors contributing to regional tourism development emanates from the region itself, that is, the tourism planner. The final tourism planning was deduced and decided on the basis of regional tourism resources, which served as the center, subject and direction. Therefore tourism development in this stage was called the resource-oriented tourism development.

5.3.1.2 Market-Oriented Tourism Development Mode

After the entry into the 1990s, with the further development of the tourism industry, every region in China began to realize the importance of developing regional tourism. Under the market mechanism, the first and foremost starting point of a tourism development mode should be the demands of the tourism market and the potential demands are more important than the actual demands. Therefore the research on and the prediction of the potential demands had become the indispensable factor for tourism planning.

The market-oriented tourism development mode contributed to the expansion of people's understanding of tourism resources. The high economic benefits gained from the development of artificial tourist attractions made people to realize that areas without any traditional advantage such as natural scenery and humanistic resources can also gain tourism revenues and become touristic cities or tourism destinations by means of planning and constructing artificial tourism products to satisfy the needs of the market. The market-oriented tourism pattern emphasizes on the exploitation of what is demanded by the market instead of the exploitation of the available resources.

5.3.1.3 Product-Oriented Tourism Development Mode

Product orientation is actually a comprehensive orientation, that is, the integration of the market orientation and resource orientation. Concerning the mode, the main work starts from the analysis and research of the market, followed by the confirmation of the targeted market by subdividing the market, later the screening, processing or recreating the regional tourism resources according to the targeted market, and finally creating, designing, producing tourism products suitable for the market through various marketing means. Under the guidance of the market, the analysis and evaluation of tourism resources can not only be professional but also be standard and scientific, which can fully enable the transfer of tourism resources to economic benefits. In order to achieve this goal, its basic idea is to evaluate, screen and process the tourism resources according to the market needs, and then design, make and combine the tourism products which are suitable for selling and promotion to the market. This way of planning represents a circulation development which starts from the market to resource, and then to the product, and finally back to the market again.

5.3.1.4 Image-Oriented Tourism Development Mode

The development idea of image orientation actually is based on the sufficient analysis and demonstration of the tourism market and tourism resources. To accomplish this mode, the first step is to confirm the tourism image for the tourism destinations, and then to nail down tourism products and their structure according to the tourism image, to design tourism network and highlight features of tourism destinations. It is a new idea based on the analytical model of product development.

5.3.2 Tourism Development Mode with Chinese Characteristics

Compared with the rapid development of China's tourism, the research on China's tourism started relatively late, with only very few theoretical studies on tourism development modes and the classification of the tourism development modes was rather chaotic. Apart from the above mentioned tourism development modes, there still exist some other classifications.

5.3.2.1 Division According to the Successful Experiences of Each Region in Tourism Development

According to the successful experiences of each region in tourism development, there arose the Zhuhai tourism development mode, the Shantou tourism development mode, the Guizhou tourism development mode, the Sichuan tourism development mode, the Guilin tourism development mode and the Pingyao tourism development mode. They considered the regional tourism development mode as the research object (Figs. 5.1 and 5.2).

Fig. 5.1 Guilin landscape

Fig. 5.2 Pingyao ancient city

5.3.2.2 Division According to Tourists' Motive and Purpose

According to tourists' tourism motive and purpose, tourism development mode can be divided into many other types, such as the sightseeing tourism development mode, the business tourism development mode, the religion tourism development mode, the ecological tourism development mode, the agricultural tourism development mode, the industrial tourism development mode, the specific tourism development mode, the red tourism development mode, the rural tourism development mode, the urban tourism development mode and the MICE-related tourism development mode, etc.

5.3.3 Newly-Emerged Tourism Development Modes in the Recent Years

5.3.3.1 The Industrial-Cluster Development Mode: Innovation of Industrial Structure

The tourism development mode is market-oriented and they have small and medium-sized enterprises as their main body. These enterprises cluster together in the same region and collaborate to make relevant tourism products. It is a grouping behavior which is similar to many ants living in a group, adopting the crowd behavior of division of labor and cooperating to finish the same task, it is also called "ant colony economy" or "cluster economy". The mode is mainly characterized by the close cooperation and support existing among many small enterprises in production, and which eventually develops into a series of complete industrial chains, presenting the phenomenon of "small enterprises, big cooperation".

5.3.3.2 "Green-Circulation" Development Mode: Innovation of the Production Mode

The circular economy requires the green development of tourism: with the rapid and stable development of the economy, the environmental problems are getting serious day after day, therefore it is an irresistible trend to stick to sustainable development and advocate the development mode of "circular economy". The circular economy is an economic development mode aiming to promote the coordination and harmony between human beings and the nature, which can help to solve the contradiction which had long existed between the economy and the environment, and to get to the level of a win-win situation.

5.3.3.3 "Knowledge-Based Economy" Development Mode: Innovation of Development Connotation

"Tourism intelligence industry" refers to knowledge-based or technology-based industrial clusters which consider the non-material objects as the main form, including management consulting, planning and design, scientific and technological development and theoretical research, etc. This product is in the form of information symbol which uses characters and graphs to express decision-making, judgment or thought.

5.3.3.4 "Emotional Exchange" Development Mode: Innovation of Investment Content

Being a special service industry, tourism not only should satisfy tourists' need for respect but also help to relieve tourists' mental pressure when a tourism product is being used by them. In the course of tourism activities, emotional exchange becomes an indispensable part of any tourism product. After the people's demand for material life is met, their spiritual demands become increasingly prominent, for this reason, the emotional exchange becomes an essential component which cannot be ignored in tourism planning.

5.4 Development Experience of China's Tourism Industry Over the Past 40 Years

After 40 years of reform and opening-up based on scientific development and continuous innovation and its own national conditions, China's tourism industry has drawn the attention of the world not only for its rapid development and great achievements, but also for the unique tourism development path with Chinese characteristics.

5.4.1 Stick to Government-Led Development Strategy, Coordinate and Utilize Social Resources and Actively Develop "Grand Tour" Industry with High Correlation and Strong Comprehensiveness

The socialist market economy requires the society to operate with high coordination, optimize the allocation of resources in all aspects, the market to grow sufficiently and the market system to be mature correspondingly. The development of China's tourism which is different from that of economically-advanced countries and some developing countries, has created a harmonious development model having the following features: government orientation, support from various departments, market as subject, operation among enterprises, social participation, coordination of benefits. The government-oriented development strategy is shown clearly in the establishment of China's outstanding touristic cities.

5.4.2 *Insist on Serving the Overall Situations, Comprehensively Perform Industrial Functions and Promote Economic and Social Improvement*

Over years of development, China's tourism was subjected to and served for the nation's political situation, economic and trading situations, diplomatic situation and the people's livelihood. Since the early stage when it served for the national opening-up, tourism demonstrated the characteristic of "folk diplomacy". Later, tourism served for the nation's economic development and earned foreign currency for the importation of foreign goods, materials and technology which were badly needed by the country. In the late 1990s, tourism played a critical role in diplomacy for a long while due to China's role as a major tourism destination for inbound travelers. When the state interests were endangered, the tourism industry gave up its industrial interest voluntarily. For example during the period of the SARS (Severe Acute Respiratory Syndromes)[1] epidemic in 2003, tourism activities were stopped throughout the nation so as to prevent the plague from spreading. With 40 years of development, the functions of tourism have expanded rapidly, from the important channel of folk diplomacy in the early stage to an important foreign exchange earner, and then to performing the comprehensive social functions. With the gradual improvement and upgrade of the industry, tourism has become the most powerful industry in terms of economic growth, a harmonious industry which propels social progress, the forerunner industry that establishes ecological civilization and boosts the coordinated development of all regions and the window industry which helps to deepen the opening-up of the country.

5.4.3 *Insist on Deepening the Reform, Strive for Exploring the New Working Fields and Drive the Innovation and Development of Tourism*

For the past three decades, China's economic society has witnessed significant changes and changes can equally be found in the economic system, administrative system and state property management system, which have directly driven the

[1]SARS, short for severe acute respiratory syndrome, is a fatal infectious disease which struck mainland China in early 2003, bringing devastating damage to the country's tourism industry, catering industry and so on.

reform of tourism management system. Tourism has developed from rigid control over all aspects of tourism affairs to transferring various kinds of autonomy rights to lower levels of administration: from direct management of the minority of tourism companies to control over the industry with streamlined administration and delegated power; from mainly state-owned system to promoting the building of modern enterprise system in tourism industry. In this process, due to the high level of openness of tourism, market mechanism has become the significant power of driving the institutional reform and institutional construction of tourism. For example, the hotel industry from the very beginning operated by following the international conventions, and the introduction of hotel management companies had directly driven the integration of the domestic and international management system. After China's entry into the WTO, in the areas of market access and citizen treatment most especially, China's tourism has realized the overall and fundamental reform and opening-up by treating enterprises of various kinds of ownership as well as foreign and domestic investments as equals.

5.4.4 *Insist on the Wider Opening-Up, Accelerate Acting on International Convention and Gradually Realize the Goal of a Powerful Nation*

Being the earliest field to open up to the outside world in China, the tourism industry had entered the international system through opening-up from the very beginning and strove for operation with international rules and conventions, which ensured its operation at the highest starting point and had laid a good foundation for the development of all fields of the industry. This kind of opening-up and integration contributed to the establishment of China's new image internationally and let to the further implementation of its reform and opening-up. The development of china's tourism has also enhanced the development of international tourism, which can be seen in the rising role of China's tourism in the world's tourism industry and its continuously increased number of outbound tourists. China has also made great contributions to the inbound tourism of many other countries in the world as an important tourism-generating country. In the world tourism economy, China's tourism has certain advantages but it still has to strive to reach the active role and the leading role. China as the world's biggest tourism nation, is required to build big tourism enterprises and nurture large tourism groups to participate in international competition. In order to build the country into a global strong tourism nation and gain a bigger market share, it is necessary for China to attract adequate foreign tourism capital, to form a batch of multinational touristic corporations and adapt to the development trend of globalization.

5.4.5 Stick to Market-Orientation, Strengthen Tourism Publicity and Sales Promotion and Improve China's Overall Image as Tourism Destination

Sticking to market orientation; exploiting tourism resources by centering on the market needs; promoting new products based on the market requirements and mapping the market is the top priority for tourism development. Tourists are the source of tourism earnings and the expansion of market scale is the base of tourism development. The tourism industry attaches great importance to the coordination and cooperation of the central and local governments in the market development. In the overseas marketing most especially, the central government and local government ought to work together in order to optimize resources and promote the entire image and products of China's tourism. Firm connection between the government and the tourism enterprises is also required. To be more specific, the government is responsible for image promotion and the enterprises are responsible for the sales promotion of products so as to carry out the developmental effect of the tourism market and gain the actual result. In order to enrich the marketing approaches of tourism, more modernized methods and increased technical means should be adopted to improve the promotion effect of tourism instead of just attending fairs and holding introductory conferences. Emphasis should be also attached to the shaping of the entire image of China's tourism. With the overall progress of China's society and the improvement of tourism facilities, the image of China as a tourism destination has been improved substantially in the minds of tourists.

5.4.6 Insist on Continuously Improving the Tourism Security System and Tourism Security Capacity by Relying on the Development of Economy and Society

Over the past 40 years, with the government endeavors at all levels and through a combination of measures such as legal, political, economic and information means, various kinds of domestic and international capital was mobilized to effectively solve the shortage of tourism supply. After the improvement of a series of infrastructure including aviation, railway, road, water transportation, electricity, communication and energy, travel and operating conditions have increasingly been improved. The supply system of China's tourism has been basically completed. With the continuous, rapid and healthy development of China's national economy, its people's tourism consumption ability is becoming more and more powerful, the consumption patterns have been more diversified and the expectation of tourism supply is growing higher. More so, the accommodation facilities and guarantee of tourism have been increased not only in quantity but it has been improved into a new stage in terms of structure and quality.

5.4.7 Insist on Improving the Service Level and Quality, Propel Tourism Standardization and Improve on the Comprehensive Competitiveness of the Tourism Industry

Quality is very important to any industry. In terms of service quality, there is still a gap between China's tourism and the tourism in the other developed countries, this influenced the improvement of comprehensive competitiveness of China's tourism industry. Service quality has become the focus for tourism management and various kinds of tourism enterprises. Years of experience have proven that the service function of tourism in the market can be perfected by adopting market-oriented concepts and standardized methods to study and improve service quality. The tourism industry of China emphasizes on learning international experiences and importing international management mode and is taking a series of corresponding measures to improve the entire service quality of the tourism industry. For example, the creation of a system table for tourism standardization technology indicates that the professional scope and management regulations have been recognized by the tourism industry in China. Anyhow, a series of standards including national standards, industrial standards, local standards and enterprise standards are required to be enriched and further improved.

5.4.8 Insist on Developing Tourism Through Science and Education, Reinforce Talent Cultivation and Technology Progress and Continuously Improve the Quality of the Tourism Industry

Tourism is the active advocate and user of modern science and technology, and tourism productivity can be improved continually through applying the new technology. China's hotel industry is the earliest industry that had made good use of electronic information system for management and the booking system adapted itself to the international practice right from the beginning. The application of digital information technology gradually expanded and a batch of digital scenic spots, digital hotels and digital tourism operation businesses emerged. The competition of tourism development also entails the competition of talents, therefore, tourism development emphasizes on the training of talents on one hand and the creating of mechanism that encourages the distinction of the various talents. For the past 40 years, China has gradually established the institutional education and adult education system for the tourism industry. The scale of tourism education and the number of trainees has emerged as the top in the world, there has been a continuous achievement in the international advanced education and the communication and cooperation with overseas education and training has been intensified. Some measures taken in the field of human resources management by tourism are envisaged for the future. Some examples of some achievements are as follows: the contract system was first carried out by Sino-foreign joint hotels, tourist guides required to take examinations to get qualified license before they start working, and the tourism industry insists on holding training classes for directors of tourism bureaus. Researches on tourism have played a major role in government decision-making and enterprise development. Scholars in tourism-related industries go deep into the industry and provide consultancy about development strategies, pushing forward the development of the industry.

5.4.9 Stick to Strict Protection and Scientific Utilization, Give Full Play to Resource-Saving and Environment-Friendly Industry and Promote the Transformation in the Development Mode of the Tourism Industry

In terms of China's tourism development, nowadays, from the central government to local governments, from government to enterprises, increasing emphasis is laid on the scientific nature of decision-making and the avoidance of detours and mistakes in exploitation, construction and management etc. Plans and guidance have played an important role in the astounding development of the tourism industry. Various regions in China have attached great importance to planning and many have put forward the concept of "construction only after planning, no construction without planning", which provides a scientific guidance to the sustainable development of tourism. The development of tourism has in turn promoted the protection of natural landscapes, historical and cultural relics, and the tourism environment has gradually become more comfortable and pleasant. In China, more natural and cultural landscapes have been listed in the World Heritage List and their popularity and influence is continuously improving; the intangible cultural heritages have achieved effective protection; more social tourism resources have been making good use of folk customs, unique life style, festival activities and traditional etiquettes have been protected and inherited. During the development of China's tourism industry, environmental protection and cultural prosperity and sustainable development are still the top priorities. Environment and culture are the foundations of tourism development, and the environmental and cultural protection is actually the protection of fundamental interest of tourism itself. Therefore, reinforcing the environmental protection of tourism destinations and establishing cultural diversity is the top priority for tourism development. Therefore, promoting environmental protection and cultural diversity, forming protection mechanism, transforming the development modes from extensive to intensive and pursuing the sustainable development are the precious experience which can never be neglected for the long-term development of the tourism industry.

5.4.10 *Stick to "People First", Advocate Social Responsibility and Promote the Scientific Development of the Tourism Industry*

China's tourism development is aimed at meeting people's increasing needs of tourism consumption and promoting people's overall progress and development. The word "people" here does not merely refer to tourists or modern people but to people as a whole, including contemporary people and their descendants, such as tourists and potential tourists, tourism developers and all interest groups related to tourism development. Tourism development embodies the spirit and connotation of "people first". Tourism development should be responsible for sustainable utilization of resources, for tourists' rights and interests, for interests of people's livelihood. Advocating social responsibility is aimed at guiding the tourism industry to not only focus on its own benefit but also on the public interests and create a more harmonious development environment. For the past 40 years, tourism as a public product, part of its properties has been realized and its public welfare awareness has been strengthened gradually, such as tourism enterprises' donations to charity, the free open of parts of urban parks and red-tourism attractions and all national museums, which certainly can promote the further development of the tourism industry. With the development of China's economy and society and the reinforcement of citizen consciousness, it is possible to advocate citizens' social obligations, in which responsible traveling[2] is an important component. Tourism behavior has rather powerful communication functions and a very significant role of image demonstration, especially with the increase of outbound tourists, tourists' role of showing national image and national quality is becoming increasingly obvious. In recent years, civilized tourism conventions advocated by the CNTA and the Central Civilization Office[3] have reflected the basic requirements of tourists' new tourism values. All these have boosted the scientific development of China's tourism industry.

Tourism has both economic and social functions and its advantages are distinct. Combining traditional and modern, productivity and life characteristics, labor-intensive, capital-intensive and knowledge-intensive, the tourism industry is an industry with striking comparative advantages in China. Since the reform and opening-up, china has made remarkable achievements in tourism. However, compared with most developed tourism nations, it should be noted that there is still much room for China's tourism to improve when taking into consideration the ever-increasing tourism needs, the goal of being a world tourism power. The gap lies mainly in the shortage of tourism legislation and industry policy; the overlapping and intersection of tourism management functions; the under-investment in the tourism public

[2]Responsible tourism includes many types of travel, all of which aim to minimize tourism's negative impacts on the environment, and maximize the positive contributions tourism can make to local communities. It is about designing tourism programs and individual trips carefully, to provide travelers with the experience they seek, while leaving a positive footprint at their destination.

[3]The Central Civilization Office, is an official organization responsible for the promotion of moral and ethic progress in China.

service; the low concentration of the tourism industry; the low international competitiveness of tourism enterprises; the weaknesses existing in the tourism service quality and human resources, etc. China's tourism started at a low level with a rather weak foundation in the software and hardware. Some other problems also emerged in the course of rapid development. Among these problems, some were periodical while some were complicated and long-lasting they had gradually been solved in the course of development.

5.5 Choice of Future Development Road for China's Tourism Industry

During the transitional period of China's economy, its tourism industry complied with the economic tide of marketization, globalization and it is also required to find proper development modes. With the degree of marketization that has become increasingly higher, it is necessary to weaken the leading role of the government. With the transformation of the industrial function and industrial policy of the tourism industry, the tourism development mode of the day is now in accordance with the time and market-oriented. This mode is oriented towards market adjustment, that is, the market decides on the direction of the flow of resources and elements through the change of supply-demand relationship. In the global market, the development of international tourism or domestic tourism is no longer decided by government policies but rather by necessity. The role of government lies in making up for market deficiency and it only plays an assistant role in tourism development.

Concerning the choice of the tourism development mode, firstly, the deciding of the urban tourism development mode shall be practicable in space. Investigation needs to be made at different forms and levels of the tourism space so as to facilitate the structural analysis of tourist behaviors and tourism behaviors from geographic space so as to help on the decision concerning the urban tourism development mode. Secondly, due to the difference in the different types of tourism activities provided by different cities and the difference in tourism supply such as tourism attractions, facilities and service etc., it is not necessary for different cities to share the same tourism development mode. To be more specific, there should be a tendency of differentiation in urban tourism development modes.

References

Department of Personnel, Labor and Education with China National Tourism Administration (1993) Introduction to Tourism. China Travel and Tourism Press, Beijing

Song Z (2006) Researches on China contemporary tourism development. Economic Management Press, Beijing

Tian L (2004) Tourism economics. Science Press, Beijing

Chapter 6
Development Policy, Prospective and Investment Outlook of China's Tourism Industry

The tourism industry is a modern emerging industry that had developed rapidly in the world. During a long period of time, China insisted on the general development guideline of "strive to develop inbound tourism, actively develop domestic tourism and moderately develop outbound tourism". After 40 years of development since the reform and opening-up, China has grown from a weak tourism country to a bigger tourism industry and it is also developing into a powerful tourism country. With the steadily rising international tourism and a continuously rising domestic tourism, the tourism industry has maintained a rapid pace in development and it plays a prominent role in the national economic development. This chapter gives a systematic discussion and analysis of China's tourism development policy and prospects, the development prospective and investment in China's tourism industry.

6.1 Policy Concerning China's Tourism Development

China's tourism development follows this order: From inbound tourism to domestic tourism and then to outbound tourism. Changes on tourism orientation reflects the change on the nation's tourism status and tourism function, and clearly explains different phases of its tourism environment and different basic policy for China's tourism industry.

6.1.1 Policy Concerning Domestic Tourism

Since the 17th CPC National Congress, in order to carry out the people-oriented outlook on social development and achieve the goal of building an overall harmonious society, domestic tourism had become a top-priority compared with inbound and outbound tourism in the national policies.

© Social Sciences Academic Press and Springer Nature Singapore Pte Ltd. 2019

P. Zhou, *The Theory and Practice of China's Tourism Economy (1978–2017)*,
Research Series on the Chinese Dream and China's Development Path,
https://doi.org/10.1007/978-981-32-9107-2_6

6.1.1.1 Main Content of Policies Concerning China's Domestic Tourism

(1) According to the official document "Suggestions Concerning the Active Development of Domestic Tourism" (1993), "In order to promote the development of domestic tourism, it is very important to give full play to the initiative of the nation, different regions, different levels of departments and individuals. Domestic tourism shall be enlisted in the development planning for national economy and society. The establishment of the domestic tourism market with unified openness and fair competition, developing mass tourism products, improving quality and protecting tourists' interests are all required. Tourism safety is an important guarantee of tourism development. Tourism administrative departments are responsible for coordinating the work related to domestic tourism."

(2) The "Outline of the Eleventh Five-Year Plan for China's Tourism Development" (2005) issued by the CNTA points out that: (1) It is necessary to reinforce the establishment of domestic tourism products system and to open up new tourism spots for domestic tourists so as to reinforce the construction of tourism facilities for residents living at the suburbs of the central cities so as to attract them to spend their weekends and holidays. The arrangement of domestic tourism activities during the time of festivals ought to be equally reinforced. There should be a strife for the development of rural tourism and reinforce the flexible supply of tourism destinations. Secondly, it is necessary to increase investment in publicizing domestic tourism and strengthen the transportation network between tourism generating places and tourism destinations and also enhance the guidance on tourism enterprises and the organization of domestic tourism promotion activities. Thirdly, it is necessary to reinforce the construction of tourism agencies running domestic tourism business and strengthen business cooperation and coordination between cities and villages on the development of the two-way tourism. Fourthly, it is necessary to further reinforce the construction of domestic tourism management system. This mainly includes perfecting the management networks, continuously enhancing the management methods and measures, formulating a series of excellent facility standards and service quality standards for domestic tourism to improve the authority and cohesion of tourism management.

6.1.1.2 Development Trend of Domestic Tourism Policy

China's domestic tourism policy is generally determined by the national macroeconomic development trend and the trend of tourism development itself. The future development of the domestic tourism policy ought to be adopted according to the development and change of these two trends. Therefore, under the new historical conditions and environment, the domestic tourism policies of promoting consumption, stimulating domestic demand and improving the quality of leisure and quality of life has been strengthened. In addition, the current China's domestic tourism policy takes into consideration the development of domestic tourism to the extent that domestic tourism can fully play the role of stimulating domestic demand and further developing the comprehensive functions of tourism. Giving priority to the development of domestic tourism can also help to increase employment opportunities and alleviate employment pressure.

6.1.2 Inbound Tourism Policy

The enforcement of relevant laws and regulations and policies of inbound tourism has promoted the rapid development of China's inbound tourism and has led to the outstanding position of inbound tourism in the early development of the industry.

6.1.2.1 Main Content of the Policy for Inbound Tourism

In order to promote the development of tourism, the Chinese government had released a series of laws and regulations since the 1950s. Here are some important laws and regulations. The first was the "Report on Reception of Foreign Travelers for Gaining Foreign Exchange and Future Suggestions" released in 1957. The report pointed out that it was necessary: to designate some high standard hotels for the reception of foreign guests and travelers at their own expenses in every major city; to open some tourism spots, including places of interest, industrial construction, agricultural cooperatives and cultural undertakings and other places that can be open to the outside world; according to the international practice, the Ministry of Railways, Civil Aviation Administration and Ministry of Communications shall give a 50% discount of transportation fee to international travelers using travel agencies at their own expenses, and will also reduce or remit charges within a certain mileage; customs, banks and relevant organizations shall also offer convenience to travelers when dealing with issues like visa application, tax levy and currency exchange and etc.

The second is the "Report on Developing China's Tourism" in 1964. According to this report, the task of developing China's tourism was to publicize achievements of China's socialist construction, expand political influence to the outside world, enhance mutual understanding and friendships between Chinese people and people in all other parts of the world and collect foreign exchange capital for the nation's economic development.

The third is the "Report on Some Issues Concerning the Vigorous Development of Tourism" released in 1979. In order to strengthen the research on the international tourism market and the connection with travel agencies in other countries or regions, China's tourism bureau headquarter was allowed to establish travel agencies in the United States, Japan, Western Europe, and Hong Kong (Fig. 6.1).

The fourth is the "Temporary Management Methods on Setting up Travel Agencies Abroad" released in 1990. The travel agencies set up abroad have as duty to: actively develop tourism business activities through a variety of means, investigate and study

Fig. 6.1 The Victoria Harbor of Hong Kong

international tourism markets, acquire tourism information, promote sales, constantly open up new tourism markets, expand the cooperation with foreign travel companies, attract more tourists to China and increase foreign exchange.

The fifth is "Request on Issues Concerning Strengthening Management of the Tourism Industry" released in 1991. Tourist product is the important component of tourism and is also one of the important ways of earning foreign exchanges. Restrictions and bans were released on the value of purchase to foreign tourists, and specific issues were to be determined by the CNTA with the Ministry of Economy and Trade.

The sixth is "Several Suggestions Concerning the Further Development of Holiday Tourism" released in 2000. The document made it clear that it was necessary to pay attention to developing inbound tourism and strive for a harvest from international tourism and domestic tourism. It was necessary to continue implementing the rapid development of inbound tourism determined by the State Council, develop domestic tourism actively, appropriately develop general policy for outbound tourism, properly handle the relationship between domestic tourism and inbound tourism and insist on giving priority to inbound tourism development so as to ensure sustained rapid growth of the number of inbound tourists and international tourism receipts, as well as the harmonious development between international tourism and domestic tourism.

The seventh is the "Notice on Further Speeding up the Development of Tourism" released in 2001. According to this Notice, active measures were to be taken so as to vigorously develop inbound tourism. On the basis of consolidating traditional tourism-generating markets, it was necessary to develop new tourism markets, strive for an increasing number of overseas tourists, and further enhance the publicity of domestic tourism markets and strengthen their image publicity in the international market. It was necessary to adopt new ways and explore new channels to continue enhancing the attraction of China's tourism in the international market. The Notice also required that the strengthening support for tourism was to be intensified so as to further increase capital investment in the development and promotion of tourism market, the way of collection of tourism development fund and its management was to be improved- these funds were to be mainly use for the development of international markets. Furthermore, the Notice insisted on the improvement of tourism transportation conditions, facilities and services of the main international scheduled flights and to gradually to increase international and domestic routes. Entry and exit procedures for international tourists were to be made easier, and short-term visa or visa upon arrival policies to international tourists were to be studied and implemented.

The eighth is the "Outline of the Eleventh Five-Year Plan for China's Tourism Development" released in 2005. According to the Outline, the development strategy and direction of China's tourism market was to strive to develop inbound tourism, standardize and develop outbound tourism, comprehensively develop domestic tourism. The Outline also insisted on the development of inbound tourism which was the key point for the development of the tourism market during the period of the 11th five-year plan. Accelerating the development of inbound tourism called for the innovation of the development mode and institutional innovation and the improvement of consumption structure for tourists traveling to China. On the basis of continuous increase of the number of inbound tourists, it was necessary to prolong tourists' stay and improve the level of consumption of tourists visiting China. Concerning the development of inbound tourism, attention was to be paid to the structural segment of tourism market and the differences existing in all types of markets, and to also make feasible marketing plan and measures according to the characteristics of the market segment. It also emphasized on the necessity to develop new potential markets while at the same time continuing to consolidate original markets.

The "Guiding Opinions on Vigorous Development of Inbound Tourism" released in 2007. In this guiding opinion, it was stated that: (1) Vigorous development of inbound tourism still remained the aim of tourism work; the system and mechanism of the development of inbound tourism shall be improved; the policy environment shall be more beneficial and inbound tourism shall healthier and orderly and there shall be a continuous and rapid development. (2) The focal points concerning the work on the rapid development of inbound tourism was to be made clear. To be more specific, this included strengthening market research and the constant mastery of the development trend of the international tourism market; the publicity and promotion of the national image had to be strengthened; the level of tourism supply to increase the attraction of inbound tourism had to be improved; perfect supporting services to improve facilitation of inbound tourism had to be established; e-commerce had to be developed and network marketing had to be improved so as to increase the level of tourism information technology; international and regional cooperation which had as objective to expand the development space of inbound tourism was to be enhanced, and the training of talents had to be intensified.

"Opinions on Further Accelerating the Development of Tourism Industry" released in 2007. According to this Opinion, it was necessary to attach great importance to inbound tourism, strengthen the effectiveness of the development of inbound tourism market, and finally explore and establish the evaluation mechanisms for market development and evaluation benefits.

6.1.2.2 Development Trend of Inbound Tourism Policy

Strengthening the policy making for international marketing and establishing a tourism image are the key development trend for China's inbound tourism policy. The Beijing Olympics of 2008 and the Shanghai World Expo of 2010 have vigorously increased the attraction and recognition of China as a tourism for international tourists. This has also been helpful in improving the image of China's tourism. At a period when countries all over the world are suffering from financial crises and are continuously witnessing natural and man-made disasters, in order to pursue self-protection, the primary goal of a country's tourism policy should be the giving of priority to its domestic tourism so as to expand the domestic consumption demand of the country. However with the economic globalization trend and the improved and advanced means of transportation, the policy of active development of inbound tourism has definitely become a long-term development strategy, whose importance cannot be undermined especially in the short-term environmental changes. Actively maintaining flexibility of policy adjustment and developing inbound tourism also helps to enable inbound tourism policy play a more comprehensive role.

6.1.3 Outbound Tourism Policy

In the mid the 1980s, China witnessed the beginning of its outbound tourism, however the actual development of the outbound tourism started in the 1990s. China's outbound tourism was characterized by the strong policy influence, particularity and complexity, which distinguish it from inbound tourism and domestic tourism.

6.1.3.1 Content of Outbound Tourism Policy

China's outbound tourism policy has gone through four stages, namely, "the policy vacuum", "the moderate development", "the standardized development" and "the orderly development".

(1) The stage of policy vacuum

After the reform and opening-up, China's economic system had experienced great changes, and accelerating economic development has been its main goal. In order to earn more foreign exchange to support national modernization construction, China had started the rapid development of its inbound tourism. During this period, the development of outbound tourism was not supported by the government. On August

13, 1984, the State Council issued a document which discouraged its citizens from traveling abroad at their own expenses. The government pointed out that for the time being it was not suitable to support its citizens to travel abroad due to the country's low economic development level and the inability to provide for the vast majority of people due to the low level of economic resources. On May 11, 1985, the State Council released provisional regulations for the management of travel agencies. These provisional regulations were divided into three categories and none was targeted towards the outbound tourism businesses. From the time the outbound tourism emerged, controlling measures had been taken by the government to regulate the market, the development scale, the supervisory measures etc. The aim of doing so was to reduce the loss of foreign exchange since at that time, the tourism industry was closely linked to the earning of foreign exchanges in the country.

(2) The stage of moderate development of outbound tourism

When the "moderate development of outbound tourism" policy was proposed, China was at the stage of allowing its citizens to travel abroad at their own expenses. At that time, the country still emphasized on reducing the loss of foreign exchange, and there were still a lot of limitations for citizens who wanted to travel abroad for any purpose. This shows that the development level of outbound tourism was not high. Policies were formulated to pursue a healthy, orderly, appropriately controlled and well organized outbound tourism market so as to fully control the qualification, quantity and quota of travel agencies that run outbound tourism businesses by means of organizing travel groups. The main specific management measures were shown in the following three aspects: (1) A limit was set on the number of outbound tourism destinations (2) A limit was set on the operational qualification for outbound tourism, (3) A limit was set on the procedure, formality and other administrative processing for outbound tourism. The implementation of the strategy of "moderate development of outbound tourism" had played an important role in exploring and accumulating experiences for outbound tourism development as well as guaranteeing healthy an orderly development of outbound tourism.

(3) The stage of standardized development of outbound tourism

The policy of "moderate development of outbound tourism" played an active role at the early stage of the development of China's outbound tourism. The so-called "standardized development of outbound tourism" policy involves the development of outbound tourism according to the inherent rules of market economy and codes of conduct determined by laws and regulations. When analyzing this policy, one can notice that the rapid development of China's outbound tourism market is actually an inevitable trend, which cannot be deliberately stopped. However, in terms of the development of outbound tourism, the core of the policy still maintained the position of no encouragement and no restriction.

(4) The stage of orderly carrying out of outbound tourism policy

In early 2009, outbound tourism in China entered into a new development stage, and the policy taken was meant to carry out outbound tourism orderly. With the increasing number of travel agencies for outbound tourism; the substantial increase of outbound tourism destinations; the wide acceptance of market-oriented management mechanism and the rate of industry competition, in order to protect rights and interests of outbound tourism consumers and travel agencies running outbound tourism businesses, the CNTA put in place the policy of orderly development of outbound tourism.

6.1.3.2 Development Trend of Outbound Tourism Policy

Just over the past ten years of development, China has become the largest tourist exporting country in Asia. Concerning the policy for outbound tourism development, the previous policy of planned and restricted development was changed into the policy of no restriction and meeting the needs. More so, the previous policy which focused on controlling the total number of outbound tourists and adjusting the number of outbound tourists to that of inbound tourists was changed into the policy which is market demand-oriented, realistic and pragmatic. In terms of policy guidance which is similar to the attitude adopted by other countries towards the development of outbound tourism, China also adopted the policy of no encouragement and no restriction. At the same time, China endeavored to enhance the international competitiveness of its own tourism enterprises by introducing positive interaction between the market and industry and taking advantage of the development of outbound tourism market. Therefore China as a big tourism country, in order to become a tourism power, its mentality which greatly influenced its previous policy on outbound tourism development had to be changed. The marketization and liberalization mechanisms for outbound tourism must be taking into consideration in the future formulation of its tourism policy.

6.2 Prospect of China's Tourism Development

The tourism industry serves not only as an important part in the social and economic life, but it also serves as a link in the industrial structure. Therefore, the prospect of the tourism industry is not only closely associated with the entire society and economy, but also with the evolution of the hierarchy in the industrial structure. Consequently, it should be examined within the framework of industrial development.

6.2.1 As Far as the Development Conditions Are Concerned, China's Tourism Industry Will Maintain Rapid Growth in the Future

This is so because: (1) China is intensifying the tapping of its tourism resources, especially the resources in the Western part of the country. The development of tourism resources in the West will become a new growth point for China's tourism industry in the future. (2), the active involvement of private capitals and foreign capitals in the tapping of tourism resources have quickened the pace of tourism resources development in China and have also added vitality to the tourism industry. (3) The improved and well-developed transportation and communication facilities and systems and the increased efforts on the improvement of the environment will vigorously help to better improve the environment for the development of the tourism industry. It will equally help to promote the development of tourism. (4) The remarkable success achieved in the readjustment of the economic structure and the obvious output of China's state-owned enterprises, will help China's economy to maintain a rapid growth in a relatively long period of time. It will also provide a strong foundation for the development of the tourism industry in future.

6.2.2 With the Adjustment and Upgrade of the Industrial Structure, the Development of the Tertiary Industry Will Gradually Step into a Rapid Developmental Stage

From the developmental stage of the industrial structure, in the course of the adjustment and upgrading of industrial structure, the development of the tertiary industry will be vigorously enhanced. According to the theory of industrial structure evolution at different stages of economic development, the development mode and the development speed of the primary industry, the secondary industry and the tertiary industry differs. At present, China is in the middle and early stage of industrialization. With the smooth progress of industrial restructuring at this stage, China's tertiary industry will gradually enter the stage of rapid development, which will provide new opportunities for the rapid development of tourism.

6.2.3 China's Consumption Level Is Moving Towards a New Stage, Which Will Create New Opportunities for Further Expansion of the Tourism Market

From the perspective of China's current consumption structure, with the continuous improvement of the people's living standard and the gradual resolution of the housing problem, people's enthusiasm for tourism would definitely intensify. After the resolution of the problem of food and clothing and with China becoming a better-off society, China's consumption level will also step into a new stage. Through the analysis of the status quo of China's economic development stage and the change in the consumption structure, it can be predicted that in the nearest future, China is expected to witness the construction of consumption hot spots in the fields of education, housing, family high-end consumer products and tourism, etc. Furthermore, with the completion of the current task in the real estate industry, the development of the tourism industry will be promoted to a higher level. When the citizens' desires for decent food and housing facilities are satisfied, they would tend to be more concerned with the desire of traveling. Therefore, tourism consumption is going to maintain a sustainable, rapid and stable growth for a very long period of time in the future, thus proving huge potential for development.

6.2.4 There Is Still a Huge Potential for Growth with China's Tourism Market

Judging from the potential of tourism market, there is still a relatively larger room for growth. From the constitution of inbound tourists, according to statistics, the majority of the tourists traveling to China's mainland were Hong Kong and Macao compatriots, as well as Taiwan compatriots which accounts for 84% and 3% respectively. The percentage of real foreigners traveling to China was just slightly more than 10%. By the end of 2000, the proportion of American tourists accounted for only 1% of the total inbound tourists, while the Japanese tourists covered merely 2.6%. The number of tourists traveling from the United States to China was less than the number of tourists travelling from South Korea and Russia respectively. In 2000, the number of the U.S. tourists traveling to China was about 8.96 hundred thousand, which is lesser than that of 1.345 million people travelling from South Korea, and 1.08 million people travelling from Russia. In the same year, the number of Japanese tourists to China was only about 2.202 million. However there is hope for a huge room for increase. With the deepening of China's opening-up to the outside world, and the active participation of foreign capital in China after China's accession to the WTO, the number of foreign tourists travelling to China is expected to rapidly grow.

6.2.5 China Has Entered into the Stage of Rapid Development in Its Domestic Tourism

Perceived from the law of development for the tourism industry, China has entered into the rapid developmental stage of its domestic tourism. Based on the law for tourism development, when a country's per capita income reaches between 500–800

US dollars, its tourism industry, especially its domestic tourism industry will enter into a very rapid stage of development. In 2000, China's per capita GDP reached a little more than 800 US dollars, with dozens of cities even surpassing 1000 dollars. Therefore, China's domestic tourism industry has every reason to expect a rapid expansion, and the development of the domestic tourism industry will certainly continue to grow with a very fast speed. Presently, the focus for the development of China's tourism industry has been gradually shifted from putting inbound tourism in the first place and domestic tourism in the second to the development of both with equal importance being attached to them. This will of course promote the future development of the domestic tourism industry.

6.2.6 The Focus of Global Tourism Is Shifting Towards the Asia Pacific, and China Will Become the Largest Tourism Destination World Over

From the change of the development mode to global tourism, the trend is that the focus of tourism is shifting towards the Asia Pacific, and China will certainly become the world's largest tourism destination. According to a forecast made by the WTO, in the next 20 years, the tourism industry in East Asia will grow at an annual rate of 7% over the region, a growth rate significantly higher than the average annual growth rate of 3.1 and 3.8% in Europe and America respectively. By 2020, the global market share owned by the European tourism industry will decline from the current 59% to 45%, while the world market share owned by East Asia Pacific's tourism industry will rise from the current 18–27%, thus excelling beyond that of America.' This will enable East Asia Pacific tourism industry to become the world's second largest tourism market.

6.2.7 China Is Basically Qualified to Build Its Tourism Industry into a World Tourism Power

It was proposed by the National Tourism Administration that China should be built into a world tourism power within 20 years. This goal is consistent with the practical requirement of China's economic and social development for tourism industry and is also in line with the forecast on the developmental prospect of China's tourism industry by the World Tourism Organization. According to this plan, by 2020, China's tourism industry will indeed become the pillar industry in its national economy, with total revenue exceeding 3.3 trillion RMB and equivalent to 8% of its GDP.

6.3 Outlook on Investment in China's Tourism Industry

Now is the right time for China to expand its investment scale in the tourism industry. There are four major factors involving to be considered in investment in the tourism industry. These are: market demand, capital supply, investment environment and optimization of project. In order to expand the scale and increase the profit in tourism investment, the following measures can be taken into consideration.

6.3.1 New Positioning

The tourism administrative departments' role in the field of investment and financing is unique; therefore, they should continue to make clear their duties and working mode. With the reform on the state investment system, tourism administrative departments' role in investment and financing should be re-positioned so as to achieve the following three major changes: Firstly, it is necessary to change from the direct arrangement of financing to indirect macro guidance and instruction. Secondly, it is necessary to change from the dependence on administrative measures to market-oriented measures. The market demand for tourism is the driving force for stimulating investment and financing, and the basis for tourism administrative departments to establish the macro guidance system. With the huge social resources, it is impossible for the traditional planned tourism to effectively guide the operation of capital for the whole industry; therefore, a new guidance mechanism ought to be built so as to adapt to the market economy. Also more coordination, guidance, planning and other indirect policy instruments should be adopted to promote tourism investment and financing. Thirdly, it is necessary to change from the administrative management to the offering of service to the whole industry.

In the new-type of investment and financing market, the role of tourism administrative departments needs to be changed from capital management to the establishment of investment and financing markets and guidance mechanisms. It can also be changed into an institution in charge of providing services of investment and financing for all parties concerned, including organizing seminars for investment projects, holding fairs, sorting out and analyzing data and information, coordination and policy research, and determining key tourism projects, etc. Being the major channels for administrative departments to guide social investment in tourism, all these services are important to the whole industry, and also very important to tourism investment and financing.

6.3.2 New Policy

The business of investment and financing is related to fiscal funds and social funds. The tourism industry in China had largely been relying on fiscal funds for a relatively long period of time; in terms of social funds, the industry relies more on the money market, and less on the capital market. Presently, with the diversified capital channel, and the soared investment demand, more concern should be focused on policies which are helpful to the tourism industry in the raising of funds through multiple channels. Most of the funds come from the non-governmental organizations, tourism enterprises, overseas investment institutions. The government also grants certain financial aid as well as priority for funds directed towards the development of the tourism market. More so, policies aimed at attracting external capital should maintain certain flexibility. In general, market demand is the most important factor for attracting foreign capital and external capital. For example, if a foreign chain hotel group is allowed to choose the first hotel address in China, Beijing or Shanghai will generally be its first choice, and the major concern for making such a choice is the market condition. As far as the price of land, cooperative conditions, preferential policies and other conditions are concerned, Beijing and other big cities have no advantage over other places, but its market location is better than that of other places.

When market demand and other conditions are the same, policy preferences have their appeal. In order to attract foreign investment, China is faced with competition not only from other Asian countries, but also from different parts of the country itself, therefore, a certain level of flexibility should be maintained in the policy. For instance, China can learn from Singapore by adopting a negotiation-for-conditions mode to attract multinational groups and chain enterprises to invest in China's tourism industry.

6.3.3 New Means

The new era calls for innovation in financing, and many new experiences are created in the fields of financing and investment in many places of China. These experiences are instructive and significant in the future investment and financing.

6.3.3.1 Zhejiang Mode

The tourism departments of Zhejiang province forged a "project first, capital second" mode, together with a set of practicable operation methods, that is, "planning leads to ideas, ideas to projects, project to funds". The so-called "project first" means there is no need to worry about finding investors, and what really matters is the creation of good projects. When a project is sound, it becomes easier to find an ideal investor.

For the preparation of a project, the focus is laid on the thorough study of the exploitative conditions, the reliable input-output analysis, and the confirmation of the project supporting policies, including clear compensation for land, tax concessions, supporting fees, and specific commitments, etc. The elaborate service work done for attracting investment has attracted a lot of money, which provides a fund guarantee for the development of Zhejiang's tourism industry.

6.3.3.2 Huashuiwan Mode

Huashuiwan hot spring tourist resort is located at the suburbs of Chengdu, Sichuan province. Huashuiwan company confronted the shortage of funds and risk of failure in the exploitation of the spring at the initial stage. Drilling the hot spring normally cost 10 million yuan, but the company only had 0.5 million. If it failed to get hot spring, the company would lose all the money and other expenses. To avoid the risk, the company had created a new type of financial product and successfully obtained the start-up capital for exploitation. The company did as follows: it used the only 0.5 million yuan as the drilling project insurance, and it was up to the insurance company to provide a secured loan of 10 million yuan. According to the contract, if the hot spring could be detected, the insurance company could take the 0.5 million yuan as insurance; if the project failed, the insurance company had to pay a loss of 10 million yuan loan to the bank. Due to the creation of this new way for capital operation, Huashuiwan company successfully obtained its early exploitation funds (Fig. 6.2).

Fig. 6.2 Huashuiwan hot spring

6.3.3.3 Asset Restructuring Mode

An asset owner obtains funds for new development and realizes increment in assets through the peeling off the superior or the inferior assets, thus enhancing the expansion ability for tourism development.

6.3.3.4 "Management Plus Investment" Mode

This way of management is more often applied in the hotel industry or property management. From the perspective of the consolidation and development of relations between strategic alliances, this way of capital management should be encouraged, particularly in areas having an underdeveloped economy.

6.3.4 New System

In the future, investment will remain an important force for the promotion of the development of the tourism industry. Therefore, based on the changes in the tourism industry under the new situation, a new tourism investment service system should be established. Firstly, it is necessary to establish a specialized agency offering service to tourism investment, and to forcefully promote tourism investment and finance activities according to new concepts and new means. Secondly, it is necessary to authorize and issue a batch of tourism development projects, and give priority to their development. Based on the overall planning for the development of the tourism industry, through market measures and by relying on fiscal funds and credibility of the government, the impact of these projects on investment market can be established, and a batch of tourism bases which can gain foreign exchange earnings and generate revenues can be constructed and shaped. Thirdly, it is necessary to set up an information database for tourism development projects, in order to carry out a comprehensive data collection and analysis for the national tourism projects which are under development and construction, and to regularly publish guidance analysis report and information. The administration should make full use of the modern electronic information technology, discs with tourism project data should be made, and information platforms for investment projects should be built in the Internet. Fourthly, it is necessary to hold tourism investment seminars and project investment fairs. For instance, presently, one of the most effective and influential international fairs is the Xiamen International Trade and Investment Fair sponsored yearly by the Ministry of Commerce. The success of such a fair is mainly decided by the number of investors and tourists participating in the activity (Fig. 6.3).

If conditions are favorable, professional tourism investment fairs can be organized, and inspection on the tourism investment environment in mid-western China and counterpart investment negotiations can also be organized. Fifthly, it is necessary to encourage the introduction of the relevant policies for the tourism industry

Fig. 6.3 Xiamen international trade and investment fair

so as to create a favorable environment for investment and investment activities. In order to achieve this aim, focus should mainly lie in the following aspects: (1) To win over increased investment in tourism industry with financial funds; (2) To design projects concerning tourism infrastructure and tourism zones; (3) To stimulate the formulation of policies encouraging investment in the tourism industry; (4)To coordinate relevant departments with the formulation of preferential policies in project approval, taxation, land and other relevant issues concerning tourism; and (5) To open up international channels and external channels for capital inflows, etc.

References

Song Z (2006) Researches on China contemporary tourism development. Economic Management Press, Beijing

Wei X, Zen B (2009) Tourism policies and regulations. Beijing Normal University press, Beijing

Zhang H, Li X et al (2005) Reports on the transformation of China's tourism industry. Tourism Education Press, Beijing

Zhang G, Liu D et al (2006) China tourism development 2004–2006: analysis and forecast. Social Science Literature Press, Beijing

Chapter 7
Analysis of the Trend of Tourism Development in China

7.1 Forecast of China's Future Tourism Development

(1) In the next ten years, the global tourism industry will remain rapid growth

The World Tourism Organization predicts that the number of global tourists will keep growing by 3.8% per year until 2020, and the number of international tourists to China will reach 1800 million by 2030. The World Tourism Association also predicts that from 2010 to 2020, the number of international tourists and international tourism income will grow by 4.3 and 6.7% annually, higher than the 3% average annual growth of the world's wealth in same period. By 2020, the international tourism industry revenue will increase to $16 trillion, equivalent to 10% of the world GDP, and it will provide 300 million job opportunities, accounting for 9.2% of total global employment, which of course will further enhance its importance in the global economy.

(2) China is more and more appealing to tourists at home and abroad for its rich tourism resources and improved tourism conditions.

On the one hand, China boasts a good many of cultural and natural heritage sites. By June 2016, China's 50 natural landscape and cultural sites had been listed in the UNESCO *World Heritage List*, ranking 2nd in the world, second only to Italy. Among the sites, 30 are cultural heritages, 11 being natural heritages, 4 being natural and cultural heritage, and 5 being cultural landscapes. On the other hand, China's natural tourism resources and cultural tourism resources has not been fully developed, especially many of the resources in the Midwest of the country still remain a mystery to visitors. With the improvement of tourism conditions and the in-depth tapping of tourism resources in East China, and the exploration of tourism resources in the Midwest, China is becoming more and more attractive to international tourists.

(3) China's tourism has a huge potential for growth, and its contribution to GDP will continue to grow

© Social Sciences Academic Press and Springer Nature Singapore Pte Ltd. 2019

P. Zhou, *The Theory and Practice of China's Tourism Economy (1978–2017)*,
Research Series on the Chinese Dream and China's Development Path,
https://doi.org/10.1007/978-981-32-9107-2_7

With the deepening of China's opening up, and the rapid development of China's tourism industry in recent ten years, overall, China's domestic tourism revenue to its GDP is going up gradually (see the table below). Owing to the global economic crisis in 2008 as well as the natural disasters happened in China, such as the Wenchuan earthquake, the ice disaster in South China and so on, the proportion went downward temporarily, but it got back on normal track gradually and contributed to 4.99% of its GDP in 2015. Even though the proportion of the revenue from the tourism industry in China's GDP is gradually increasing, the current proportion is still low when compared with that of them moderately developed countries. Although the contribution of the tourism industry to China's GDP is increasing gradually, the proportion of GDP is still low when compared with that of the moderately developed countries. In those countries, the proportion of total tourism revenue to GDP accounts for about 10%, while in the countries where the tourism industry is the pillar or leading industry, the proportion of total tourism revenue to GDP is over 20%. With the increase of income for urban and rural residents and the improvement of their quality of life, especially with the increasing scale of the middle income class, the consumption expectation of tourism will be greatly stimulated, which certainly will lead to the quick expansion of tourism participants and the continuous increase of the scale of the tourism industry. According to the prediction made by the World Tourism Organization, by 2020, China will become the world's largest tourist destination, and the total tourism revenue will reach 8% of its GDP, therefore, a huge space for future growth can be expected (Fig. 7.1).

Fig. 7.1 Ruis of Wenchuan earthquake

Total Domestic Tourism Receipts to GDP (2006–2015)

Year	Total GDP (trillion yuan)	Total domestic tourism receipts (trillion yuan)	Total domestic tourism receipts to GDP (% of GDP)
2006	21.94	0.62	2.83
2007	27.02	0.78	2.89
2008	31.95	0.87	2.72
2009	34.91	1.02	2.92
2010	41.30	1.26	3.05
2011	48.93	1.93	3.94
2012	54.04	2.27	4.20
2013	59.52	2.63	4.42
2014	64.40	3.03	4.70
2015	68.55	3.42	4.99

However, the contribution of tourism to GDP is not only confined by the industry itself. In fact, this modern tourism industry is strongly integrated into and correlated with other industries, and with a long industrial chain. It has broken through scope of the traditional tourism, and has been widely involved with and intersected into many related industries and trades. According to the statistics of the World Tourism Organization, when 1 yuan is earned by the tourism industry, the other related industries can harvest 4.3 yuan. According to the calculation of Japan's Nomura Research Institute, in developed countries, when expenditure on tourism consumption increases by one unit, the industrial output value can expand by 2.71 times, the national income will expand by 1.36 times, and the investment will expand by 0.25 times. The tourism industry can influence, drive and promote the development of other 110 industries associated with it, thus employment will be increased. According to foreign scholars, the employment of one more tourism labor means an increase of 4.2 employment opportunities in other related industries.

(4) The upgrading of the structure of the tourism market: from sightseeing to leisure vacation

After several decades of rapid development, China's tourism is facing the problem of overall transformation. At present, the structure of tourism market system is still unitary, with sightseeing outshining its rivals and occupying a dominant position, be it in inbound tourism, outbound tourism or in domestic tourism. For a period of time, sightseeing will continue to maintain the largest market share, but with the emergence and gradual expansion of the middle-income class in China, the demand for more and more leisure time, and the increasing demand for high quality life, tour items for leisure and vacation will be preferred so that people can get better relaxation and more experience about life. When the time comes, leisure and vacation tourism will rise rapidly and its travel types will also diversify, while the market structure of tourism will gradually transform from sightseeing to leisure travel.

7.2 Analysis of the Trend of Tourism Development in China

In the next ten years, China's tourism industry will become more and more promising and is likely to be the locomotive of the global tourism industry. According to "China's Tourism Industry In-depth Survey and Investment Prospects Forecast Report 2017–2021", a report released by CIConsulting,[1] in the period of "13th Five-Year Plan" (2016–2020), China's tourism industry will manifest the following development trends: (1) Tourism consumption will become popular among the masses. With the development of a well-off society in an all-round way, tourism has become an important part in people's daily life. Self-help tour and self-driving tour will become the main ways of traveling. (2) A distinct trend is that quality tourism, especially tourism of medium and high quality is demanded by the masses. With the rapid growth of people's demand for leisure and vacation tourism, they have increasingly high demand for infrastructure, public services, ecological environment, as well as personalized and particular tourism products and services. (3) The overall integration of the tourism industry with other industries. The mode of tourism development is transforming quickly from merely the development of tourist attractions to that of the all-dimensional development mode, which is characterized by its integration with regional resources, industry convergence, co-construction and sharing, etc. As a result, the tourism industry is deeply integrated with other industries, such as agriculture, industry, forestry, water conservancy, science and technology, culture, sports, health care and so on. (4) The modernization of the tourism industry. The role that science and technology, culture creativity, management and top talents play on tourism development is increasing. Cloud computing, the Internet of things, big data and other modern information technologies are more widely used in the tourism industry. The modernization of the industrial system has become an inevitable trend in the development of tourism. More specifically, in a promising environment, China's tourism industry will present the following seven development trends:

First, the investment in the tourism industry is growing very fast. Over the past three decades and more, China's economy has grown by an average of 7.4%, and China now is the No. 2 biggest economy of the world. In the next decade, China will remain an important engine of global economic growth, and its tourism will be the most promising industry to invest in. There is still a huge space and potential for tourism investment, for China is entering a new stage of benign interaction and mutual promotion between tourism consumption market and tourism investment market. As one of the largest industries in the world, it is not enough for the tourism industry to merely rely on the optimal allocation of the existing resources. More effective investment from the outside is still needed. In the next decade, large capital from other industries will accelerate their pace into the tourism industry, and the trend of cross-industry investment will become more and more obvious. At the same time,

[1] With more than ten-year expertise in terms of market survey, market research, industry research and investment consulting services, CIConsulting is now a leading professional institution in the field of industry research in China.

merger and reorganization of tourism enterprises and the pace of "going global" will be accelerated, and tourism resources will be deeply integrated.

Second, the integration with other industries is the essential attribute of the tourism industry. This attribute determines that only by relying on multiple industries can it be possible for the tourism industry to provide tourists with necessary tourism products and services, including transportation, accommodation, food, travel, shopping and entertainment, etc. The correlation with other industries not only preconditions the integrated development of the tourism industry, but also widens its space for such development. Being integrated and correlated with other industries, the tourism industry is considered as a strategic industry having superiority in the national economy in terms of integrated development. Tourism is a comprehensive industry as well as an important driving force for economic development. Tourism is now becoming increasingly integrated with other industries. During China's 13th five-year plan period (2016–2020), the integration of tourism with national life as well as with other key areas such as rural leisure tour, health and old-age care, will become new hotspots for tourism development.

Third, the infiltration of tourism into the whole industrial chain of the Internet. In September 2015, the "Tourism + Internet" conference was held in Changzhou, Jiangsu province. At the meeting, the national tourism administration issued the "Tourism + Internet" action plan; meanwhile, China's "Internet + Tourism Destination" alliance released the Changzhou consensus on promoting the integration and development of "Tourism + Internet". The conference also proposed that in the next five years, China's "Tourism + Internet" is expected to generate "three 1 trillion dividends": In the next five years, the construction of Internet hardware and software facilities in China's tourism industry will create a demand dividend of 1 trillion yuan, while China's online tourism trade will generate 1 trillion yuan of market dividends. In the next five years, a large number of new technologies, new products, new business models and new models will be created, which will generate a value-added dividend of 1 trillion yuan. A series of national policies for promoting the development of the tourism industry have been issued to solve a series of problems in optimizing the allocation of tourism production factors, including land, capital, system, mechanism, organization, technology, human resources and brands, etc. At present, the Internet tourism manifests the following four development trends. First, the consumption side of tourism is undergoing five big changes: differentiation in tourist groups; enrichment in travel experience; self-service in travel design; the transaction process is being carried out by e-commerce or on-line; the rationalization of tourism shopping, i.e., the quality, origin and price of goods become the considerations of tourists in shopping. Second, in view of the current status of different subdivision of each sector of the tourism industry, there is still a lot of room for market segmentation. The integration between tourism and lifestyle will constantly expand the tourism scope, and the demand for tourism will become more and more diversified, which will further promote the integration of tourism and other industries, and further deepen the segmentation of market and consumption scenarios. The series of changes require continuous upgrading of the coverage and fineness of the Internet, and the efficient transmission of information by the Internet will continue to accelerate the maturity and efficiency of the industry pattern. Third, technology-driven enterprises will promote the in-depth exploration of product value. The tourism industry will eventually return to the tapping of product value and service value. In addition to the information technology of the Internet, the SaaS technology, the big data technology and even artificial intelligence will all contribute to the tapping and matching of client demand, the sharing of resources and the upgrading of product experience. Fourth, the online and offline integration becomes diversified. Both Internet enterprises and traditional enterprises are seeking for the integration of online and offline services. However, at present, it is more about the integration of various channels. With the penetration of the Internet in the tourism industry and on the basis of the integration of channels, the integration of online and offline services and experience under different scenarios will become more accessible to tourists.

Fourth, the supply of tourism products is shifting from "resources + land" to "investment + feelings". With the arrival of mass tourism, tourism is becoming a normal life style for ordinary people. However, at present, there are still some problems with the supply of tourism products. In the current situation, the traditional tourism products are in excess of supply, while the new tourism products are often short of supply. For example, there is a surplus of sight-seeing products while a shortage of leisure vacation, health maintenance and the elderly care products. As a result, the oversupply of traditional products has led to the spillover of demand, market investment and benefit; therefore, it is urgent to push forward the supply-side reform in the tourism industry. In the traditional profit model dominated by resources and land appreciation, investment in interest-related projects begins to play an increasingly important role, and projects like high-quality rural tourism and non-standard accommodation becomes more and more popular. Therefore, in the next decade, more and more attention will be paid to travellers' interest in tourism investment regardless of the size of the project investment. And it is suggested that the supply of tourism products should be strengthened in tourism format, tourism experience and personal service, etc.

Fifth, transforming from "small tourism" to "big tourism". In the primary stage of tourism development, the focus is mainly laid on building scenic spots, scenic zones, hotels and guesthouses, which of course is a mode of "scenic spot tourism". However, up to now tourism development has entered into a brand new stage in which mass tourism and self-driving tour are given priority. As a comprehensive industry, tourism is playing a bigger role in economic and social development, and its responsibilities have also improved notably. Hence, the traditional scenic-spot-oriented tourist model can no longer meet the development needs of "big tourism"; many places in the country have started to develop all-for-one tourism mode. The so-called "all-for-one" tourism simply means to plan and build a whole city into a tourist attraction, and to transform the tourism industry from single to a comprehensive industry, from small to big tourism, and ultimately to realize a development model entailing all regional resources, overall layout and construction, and involvement of the whole people. Judging from the current development situation of the tourism industry domestically and internationally, all-for-one tourism will become the general trend for future development of the tourism industry.

Sixth, being globalized is a distinct trend of the tourism industry. China is truly a big country in tourism and consumption, but to become a tourism power, it also needs to enhance its own supply capability and to participate in international competition. The period of the 13th five-year plan (2016-2010) is the decisive stage to build China into a moderately prosperous society in all respects, and also the decisive stage for the tourism industry to fully implement the 515 Strategy,[2] to deepen reform and promote quality and efficiency of the industry; thus, realizing the transformation of China from "a preliminarily comfortably-off tourism power" to "an overall comfortably-off tourism country". In the next decade, there will be more international tourism enterprises entering the Chinese market; meanwhile, more and more Chinese tourism enterprises will speed up their pace of going global, and China's tourism industry will be more and more globalized. For this reason, China should actively merge its tourism enterprises into the international system of the division of labor, and play an important role in it. From tourism channel to destination, China should accelerate the control of its tourism resources and compete for a greater say in international division of labor. Since tourism competition has become internationalized, places across the country generally take the development of tourism as an important means to participate in the international market division and enhance international competitiveness. Policies and measures have been introduced to promote the development of tourism, to promote the globalization of tourism market and the internationalization of tourism competition, and the field of competition has expanded from competing for tourist market to each aspect of tourism development.

Seventh, the development of tourism calls for innovation. According to a survey made globally, 69% of tourists investigated would plan new journeys in 2016, and travellers of almost all ages are seeking new travel experiences. In the next decade, with the enrichment of tourism experience, more and more people will be interested in new types of tourism, such as cruise or Rv travel, backpacking or adventure travel, etc. The demand for new types of tourism will continuously stimulate the equipment manufacturing of the tourism industry in the next decade, while innovation will certainly trigger new vitality of the tourism market (Fig. 7.2).

To sum up, tourism policies are beneficial to many other industries, and the integration of the tourism industry and other industries is diversified, with a lot of opportunities. But at the same time, the influx of non-travel capital and the strong existing tourism capital will also intensify the industry competition, and a new round of fierce competition will emerge, and only the strongest can stand out. After the competition, a "big era" of tourism with multiple tourism giants will come in the next decade.

[2]The Strategy was proposed by Li Jinzao, head of National Tourism Administration in 2015. Centering on 5 major goals, the Strategy aims to launch 10 major tourism initiatives, and to carry out 52 measures so to advance the transformation and upgrading of the tourism industry, to improve its quality and efficiency, and to speed up the modernization and internationalization of the industry in the following three years (2015–2017).

Fig. 7.2 Adventure travel in China

7.3 The Focus of China's Future Tourism Investment

At present, the main characteristics of tourism investment in China are as follows: The private investment is stable and a diversified investment pattern is basically formed; investment in scenic areas remains stable and the growth of investment in new tourism formats is accelerating; the eastern regions of the country are hot spots for investment, while the western regions witness the fastest growth in investment; continuous innovation in investment and financing modes has accelerated the development of PPP mode; industrial investment funds have been growing rapidly and new forms of investment are favored; the integration of tourism enterprises is accelerated, and investment in m&a and restructuring is noticeable. The investment in hot areas of tourism mainly include the continuous rise of rural tourism investment, the emergence of large-scale comprehensive projects as capital pets, the continuing popularity of online tourism investment, and the huge potential of new forms of investment. China's future tourism investment environment foresees a good prospect. With China's deepening implementation of its policies of "Belt and Road" initiative, urbanization, the Construction of Beautiful Countryside, mass entrepreneurship and innovation as well as the implementation of the policy of tax reduction to benefit the people, the space and fields of tourism investment are constantly expanding. The acceleration of supply-side structural reform will bring new development opportunities for the reform of state-owned tourism enterprises and the integrated development between tourism and the first, second and third industries. From the current and future development trend of China's tourism industry, the following ten fields will become important ones for future tourism investment:

First, the investment in rural tourism products integrated with leisure agriculture will see a rapid growth, such as the development of leisure farm, featured countryside, and rural boutique home stay, etc.;

Second, the investment in low-altitude tourism products, such as low-altitude tourism route, air tourism towns, low-altitude tourism aircrafts, etc.;

Third, the investment in online tourism products, including tourism Internet finance, the integration of destination tourism resources, creative tourism products, and shared tourism products, etc.;

Fourth, the investment in big tourism data and smart tourism products, including big tourism data centers, the application of big tourism data, smart tourism transportation, smart tourism administration, future scenic spots, and future hotels, etc.;

Fifth, the investment in the construction of leisure and resort products, including tourism resorts, tourism complexes, featured tourism towns, featured commercial blocks, comprehensive resort hotels, and boutique hotels, etc. (Fig. 7.3).

Sixth, the investment in cultural tourism products, such as large-scale performing arts, theme parks, cultural and creative parks, music parks, and art centers, etc.;

Seventh, the investment in sports tourism products, including competitive sports events, participatory sports events, mass sports activities, sports festivals, and ski resorts, etc.;

Fig. 7.3 A featured tourism town in China

Eighth, the investment in health care tourism products, such as traditional Chinese medicine health care bases, physical examination organizations, medical rehabilitation centers, health & holiday bases, and tourism products for the elderly, etc.;

Ninth, the investment in tourism research products, including research bases, theme museums, leisure libraries, etc.;

Tenth, the investment in a new type of tourism equipment manufacturing industry, such as cruise ships, aircrafts, recreation facilities, motor homes, wooden houses, skiing and golf equipment, etc.

Appendix A
Memorabilia of Tourism Since China's Reform and Opening-up from 1978 to 2011

In August 1982, China Administration of Travel and Sightseeing was renamed China National Tourism Administration.

In 1985, the first tourism administrative regulation, namely- *Interim Regulations on the Management of Travel Agencies*, was issued.

In October 1990, the outbound travel to Singapore, Malaysia and Thailand was for the first time opened to Chinese citizens at their own expense.

In 1995, the two-day weekend system was implemented, which promoted the development of domestic tourism to a higher level.

In 1996, the State Council of China issued the *Regulations on Administration of Travel Agencies*: it divided the travel agencies into two categories, namely the international agency and the domestic agency from the original three categories; this classification framework is still in use today.

In 1999, according to the new regulation on public holiday, a 7-days holiday was made for three big occasions, namely, the Spring Festival, the May Day Holiday and the National Day Holiday; thus, the so-called "Golden Week" came into existence.

In 2000, in order to enter the international market, *Star-rating Standard for Tourist Hotels* was formally submitted to the International Organization for Standardization. This was the first step taken towards tourism standardization; Japan, Vietnam, Brunei, Kampuchea and Burma became China's tourism destinations in the year.

In 2001, China announced the accession of the tourism industry into the World Trade Organization and made a commitment to lower the threshold so as to enable foreigners to invest in the travel agency.

In 2002, the Civil Aviation Administration of China decided to cancel all red eye flights; the memorandum of understanding which gives the authorization to Chinese nationals to go for travel was signed between China and other six countries—Germany, Russia, Sri Lanka, South Africa, Maldives, and India.

In the first three quarters of 2003, China's tourism was severely affected by the sudden outbreak of SARS. However, it was rebounded and it rapidly recovered

© Social Sciences Academic Press and Springer Nature Singapore Pte Ltd. 2019

P. Zhou, *The Theory and Practice of China's Tourism Economy (1978—2017)*,
Research Series on the Chinese Dream and China's Development Path,
https://doi.org/10.1007/978-981-32-9107-2

after the Golden Week running from Oct. 1 to Oct. 7. In Oct. of the same year, the 15th General Assembly Session of the World Tourism Organization was officially held in Beijing.

In September 2004, 29 countries in Europe were officially open to Chinese citizens for travel and the first group traveling to Europe set out.

In 2005, China's first low-cost airline—the Spring and Autumn Airlines started the first flight, marking the rise in a low-cost aviation boom; thereafter, the choice of cheap flights for traveling became common with the Chinese people.

From 2006 on, both "rural tourism" and "Tibet Tour" became popular in China; the "Village Tour" became the theme of Chinese tourism.

In 2007, the total revenue of China's tourism hit 1 trillion and reached 1.09 trillion Yuan, hence 2007 was a year marked by a significant turning point

In 2008, the *Regulation on Public Holidays for National Annual Festivals and Memorial Days* and the *Regulations of Paid Annual Leave of Employees* started to be implemented; meanwhile, the first batch of Chinese citizens traveling to the United States set out; in July of the year, traveling to Taiwan by residents from China's mainland was formally implemented.

In 2009, the new *Regulations on Travel Agencies* and the revised *Regulations on Administration of Travel Agencies* came into effect. This was also China's first eco-tourism year.

In 2010, the construction of Hainan international tourism island was officially launched; China's tourism maintained a rapid growth under the impetus of Shanghai World Expo and the Asian Games held in Guangzhou.

On May 19, 2011, the first "China Tourism Day" was launched; in June of the same year, the high-speed railway connecting Beijing and Shanghai was officially opened, and high-speed train trips had become more popular ever since; on June 28th of the same year, Mainland residents' personal travel to Taiwan was officially launched.

Appendix B
Data Tables for the Development of Tourism Economy in China

See Tables B.1, B.2, B.3, B.4, B.5, B.6, B.7, B.8, B.9, B.10, B.11, B.12, B.13 and B.14.

Table B.1 International tourism receipts 1978–2016

Year	International tourism receipts (US $ Million)	Development index (100 for 1978)	Increase against the previous year (%)
1978	2.63	100.00	
1979	4.49	170.90	70.90
1980	6.17	234.60	37.30
1981	7.85	298.60	27.30
1982	8.43	320.70	7.40
1983	9.41	358.00	11.60
1984	11.31	430.30	20.20
1985	12.50	475.50	10.50
1986	15.31	582.30	22.50
1987	18.62	708.10	21.60
1988	22.47	854.60	20.70
1989	18.60	707.70	−17.20
1990	22.18	843.50	19.20
1991	28.45	1082.10	28.30
1992	39.47	1501.30	38.70
1993	46.83	1781.40	18.70
1994	73.23	2785.40	*
1995	87.33	3321.70	19.30

(continued)

© Social Sciences Academic Press and Springer Nature Singapore Pte Ltd. 2019

P. Zhou, *The Theory and Practice of China's Tourism Economy (1978—2017)*,
Research Series on the Chinese Dream and China's Development Path,
https://doi.org/10.1007/978-981-32-9107-2

Table B.1 (continued)

Year	International tourism receipts (US $ Million)	Development index (100 for 1978)	Increase against the previous year (%)
1996	102.00	3879.98	16.80
1997	120.74	4592.67	18.40
1998	126.02	4793.36	4.40
1999	140.99	5362.70	11.90
2000	162.24	6171.17	15.10
2001	177.92	6767.59	9.70
2002	203.85	7753.90	14.60
2003	174.06	6620.82	−14.60
2004	257.39	9790.35	47.90
2005	292.96	11,143.38	13.80
2006	339.49	12,913.28	15.90
2007	419.19	15,944.81	23.50
2008	408.43	15,535.43	−2.60
2009	396.75	15,091.29	−2.90
2010	456.14	17,419.77	15.50
2011	484.64	18,434.33	5.80
2012	500.28	19,029.29	3.20
2013	516.64	19,651.40	3.30
2014	1053.80	40,083.70	*
2015	1136.50	43,229.40	7.80
2016	1200.00	45,626.50	5.60

Source Based on the statistical data released by the National Tourism Administration over the years

Note Due to the reform on the foreign currency system, the methods of calculating tourism receipts in 1994 had also been adjusted and the international standard had been adopted. Therefore, it will not be proper to make simple comparisons with the figures of the previous years.

Table B.2 International tourist arrivals according to age, sex, occupation and means of transport 2015—2016 (Unit: 10,000 Peoples)

Item	2016	P.C. total	2015	P.C. total
Total	3148.38	100.0	2598.54	100.0
14 or under	114.73	3.6	101.43	3.9
15–24	303.32	9.6	205.03	7.9
25–44	1473.56	46.8	1184.25	45.6
45–64	1078.39	34.3	949.76	36.5
65 or over	178.37	5.7	158.07	6.1
Male	1982.04	63.0	1681.19	64.7
Female	1166.33	37.0	917.35	35.3
Meeting/business	579.74	18.4	537.66	20.7
Sightseeing/ leisure	1051.15	33.4	824.88	31.7
Visiting friends and relatives	96.19	3.1	79.75	3.1
Worker and crew	471.75	15.0	349.69	13.5
Others	949.55	30.1	806.57	31.0
Sea	284.49	9.0	250.55	9.6
Air	1691.12	53.7	1557.14	59.9
Rail	41.98	1.3	45.54	1.8
Motor	442.74	14.1	324.87	12.5
Foot	688.05	21.9	420.44	16.2

Source Based on the statistical data released by the National Tourism Administration over the years

Table B.3 China international tourist arrivals and receipts (1978—2016)

Year	Overnight arrivals (million)	World ranking	Receipts (US$ million)	World ranking
1978	0.716	41	263	–
1979	1.529	31	449	–
1980	3.5	18	617	34
1981	3.767	17	785	34
1982	3.924	16	843	29
1983	3.791	16	941	26
1984	5.141	14	1131	21
1985	7.133	13	125	21
1986	9.001	12	1531	22
1987	10.76	12	1862	26
1988	12.361	10	2247	26
1989	9.361	12	1860	27
1990	10.484	11	2218	25
1991	12.464	12	2845	21
1992	16.512	9	3947	17
1993	18.982	7	4683	15
1994	21.07	6	7323	10

(continued)

Table B.3 (continued)

Year	Overnight arrivals (million)	World ranking	Receipts (US$ million)	World ranking
1995	20.034	8	8733	10
1996	22.765	6	10,200	9
1997	23.77	6	12,074	8
1998	25.0729	6	12,602	7
1999	27.0466	5	14,099	7
2000	31.2288	5	16,224	7
2001	33.1667	5	17,792	5
2002	36.8026	5	20,385	5
2003	32.9705	5	17,406	7
2004	41.7614	4	25,739	7
2005	46.809	4	29,296	6
2006	49.9134	4	33,949	5
2007	54.7198	4	41,919	5
2008	53.0492	4	408.43	5
2009	50.8752	4	396.75	5
2010	55.6645	3	458.14	4
2011	57.5807	3	484.64	4
2012	57.7249	3	500.28	4
2013	55.6859	4	516.64	4
2014	55.6220	*	1053.80	*
2015	56.8857	4	1136.50	2
2016	59.2673	4	1200.00	2

Source Based on the statistical data released by the National Tourism Administration over the years

Table B.4 Monthly international tourist arrivals 2016 (Unit: 1000 Peoples)

Month	Total	Sea	Air	Rail	Motor	Foot
Whole year	14,196.63	473.15	2267.56	113.79	3026.74	8315.39
Jan.	1110.84	34.55	158.71	8.74	244.69	664.14
Feb.	984.44	32.61	153.50	9.24	205.34	583.76
Mar.	1206.49	39.65	194.54	10.33	257.92	704.06
Apr.	1193.88	41.02	200.21	11.91	257.35	683.38
May	1162.00	39.99	194.70	9.01	247.41	670.89
June	1129.74	41.78	187.57	8.40	243.72	648.26
July	1171.38	44.06	195.02	9.29	242.74	680.27
Aug.	1122.94	41.91	193.41	8.72	236.87	642.02
Sept.	1193.63	38.46	194.81	8.87	254.37	697.12
Oct.	1309.91	42.16	223.64	10.49	268.08	756.53
Nov.	1287.87	38.59	190.22	9.11	276.38	773.57
Dec.	1332.52	38.36	181.23	9.67	291.87	811.39

Source The Yearbook of China's Tourism Statistics 2017

Table B.5 International tourist arrivals according to nationality and purpose 2016 (Unit: 10,000 Peoples)

Nationality	Total	Meeting/business	Sightseeing/ leisure	Visiting friends or relatives	Service staff	Others
Total	3148.38	579.74	1051.15	96.19	471.75	949.55
Asia	*2125.08*	*327.19*	*726.26*	*23.88*	*368.35*	*679.39*
Japan	258.74	77.79	40.19	6.17	13.45	121.14
South Korea	476.22	101.45	239.77	4.16	41.54	89.30
Mongolia	134.23	9.48	8.56	0.05	38.20	77.94
Indonesia	63.29	3.14	32.41	0.38	21.81	5.54
Malaysia	116.39	16.79	69.24	1.66	11.91	16.80
Philippines	113.47	3.22	19.99	0.29	80.61	9.37
Singapore	92.19	21.04	24.15	6.18	7.15	33.67
Thailand	74.90	4.67	42.50	0.33	20.16	7.24
India	79.91	20.91	16.01	0.36	22.73	19.91
Others	715.74	68.70	233.46	4.31	110.79	298.48
Europe	*543.99*	*160.85*	*171.59*	*13.69*	*69.84*	*128.03*
Britain	59.43	15.00	18.35	3.29	5.05	17.73
France	50.35	9.88	14.34	1.92	3.77	20.44
Germany	62.27	21.45	11.19	2.63	4.23	22.76
Italy	26.68	6.61	7.89	0.45	3.83	7.91
Switzerland	7.26	1.89	2.41	0.35	0.68	1.92
Sweden	11.52	3.43	2.75	0.80	0.86	3.69
Holland	19.95	4.46	4.74	1.18	2.21	7.37
Russia	197.60	72.96	81.47	0.45	25.77	16.94
Others	108.95	25.17	28.46	2.62	23.44	29.26
America	*337.88*	*54.72*	*118.30*	*44.50*	*22.50*	*97.86*
U.S.A	224.78	38.12	85.73	23.01	15.00	62.92
Canada	74.08	7.98	20.09	19.37	3.22	23.42
Others	39.02	8.62	12.48	2.12	4.28	11.52
Oceania	*82.35*	*14.43*	*23.70*	*13.55*	*4.18*	*26.48*
Australia	67.32	11.69	20.35	11.46	2.99	20.84
New Zealand	13.60	2.48	3.14	1.98	0.73	5.26
Others	1.42	0.27	0.21	0.10	0.47	0.38
Africa	*58.86*	*22.51*	*11.21*	*0.56*	*6.86*	*17.72*
Others	*0.22*	*0.04*	*0.09*	*0.01*	*0.02*	*0.06*

Source The Yearbook of China's Tourism Statistics 2017

Table B.6 International tourist arrivals according to nationality, age, and sex 2016 (Unit: 10,000 Peoples)

Nationality	Total	Age					Sex	
		14 or under	15–24	25–44	45–64	Over 65	Male	Female
Total	*3148.38*	*114.73*	*303.32*	*1473.56*	*1078.39*	*178.37*	*1982.04*	*1166.33*
Asia	*2125.08*	*61.43*	*222.75*	*1058.17*	*677.83*	*104.90*	*1350.15*	*774.93*
Japan	258.74	9.83	9.23	97.20	119.17	23.32	202.42	56.33
RO Korea	476.22	19.21	32.40	172.59	211.64	40.38	287.08	189.14
Mongolia	134.23	4.12	9.54	82.06	37.24	1.27	85.02	49.21
Indonesia	63.29	1.81	7.91	33.16	16.52	3.89	38.00	25.29
Malaysia	116.39	4.47	8.41	50.68	43.23	9.59	70.24	46.15
Philippines	113.47	1.28	7.67	74.39	28.50	1.64	90.15	23.32
Singapore	92.19	5.01	5.10	32.00	40.94	9.14	58.43	33.76
Thailand	74.90	1.58	5.81	39.48	22.72	5.31	34.95	39.96
India	79.91	2.08	6.36	52.07	17.72	1.69	68.92	11.00
Others	715.74	12.05	130.32	424.55	140.14	8.68	414.95	300.78
Europe	*543.99*	*19.17*	*45.95*	*242.14*	*206.71*	*30.02*	*334.10*	*209.89*
Britain	59.43	2.90	4.33	22.72	24.77	4.72	40.88	18.55
France	50.35	2.82	4.24	22.56	17.45	3.28	33.14	17.21
Germany	62.27	2.43	4.19	25.40	27.16	3.09	46.08	16.19
Italy	26.68	0.63	1.60	12.42	10.52	1.50	20.49	6.19
Switzerland	7.26	0.26	0.45	2.61	3.27	0.67	5.11	2.14
Sweden	11.52	0.60	0.84	4.31	5.00	0.76	7.80	3.72
Holland	19.95	0.84	1.63	7.82	8.45	1.21	13.40	6.54
Russia	197.60	5.61	19.49	88.30	73.81	10.39	92.12	105.47
Others	108.95	3.08	9.19	56.00	36.29	4.39	75.07	33.88
America	*337.88*	*25.51*	*24.81*	*109.35*	*143.84*	*34.37*	*206.33*	*131.54*
U.S.A	224.78	15.90	16.03	66.63	100.35	25.87	139.66	85.12
Canada	74.08	6.80	5.48	23.05	31.96	6.79	41.33	32.75
Others	39.02	2.81	3.31	19.67	11.53	1.70	25.34	13.68
Oceania	*82.35*	*7.69*	*5.70*	*27.13*	*33.70*	*8.13*	*49.43*	*32.92*
Australia	67.32	6.02	4.52	22.16	27.64	6.98	40.35	26.98
New Zealand	13.60	1.62	1.02	4.25	5.60	1.11	8.04	5.56
Others	1.42	0.04	0.17	0.71	0.46	0.04	1.04	0.38
Africa	*58.86*	*0.92*	*4.09*	*36.71*	*16.21*	*0.93*	*41.88*	*16.99*
Others	*0.22*	*0.00*	*0.01*	*0.07*	*0.10*	*0.02*	*0.15*	*0.07*

Source The Yearbook of China's Tourism Statistics 2017

Table B.7 International tourist arrivals according to locality 2016

Locality	Foreigners			Hongkong compatriots		
	Arrivals	Nights	Average stay	Arrivals	Nights	Average stay
Total	58,701,276	186,957,986	3.36	29,732,120	75,851,958	3.42
Beijing	3,547,619	15,254,762	4.30	352,942	1,517,651	4.30
Tianjin	718,904	11,105,706	15.45	52,595	1,165,959	22.17
Hebei	659,877	2,334,132	3.54	68,776	166,357	2.42
Shanxi	404,221	1,034,942	2.56	96,721	228,367	2.36
Inner Mongolia	1,682,734	4,843,653	2.88	41,466	175,717	4.24
Liaoning	2,122,140	6,052,093	2.85	265,171	707,720	2.67
Jilin	1,421,729	3,443,082	2.42	96,438	253,436	2.63
Heilongjiang	908,707	1,998,286	2.20	9961	29,651	2.98
Shanghai	5,725,655	17,945,849	3.13	477,103	1,540,922	3.23
Jiangsu	2,179,954	7,526,609	3.45	153,754	380,831	2.48
Zhejiang	3,873,006	10,160,086	2.62	469,757	1,081,053	2.30
Anhui	1,844,596	4,308,687	2.34	406,609	1,074,267	2.64
Fujian	2,541,193	13,776,126	5.42	1,336,794	6,277,606	4.70
Jiangxi	498,020	946,029	1.90	542,331	1,020,118	1.88
Shandong	2,376,575	8,369,697	3.52	406,478	1,175,245	2.89
Henan	958,064	2,096,414	2.19	206,356	394,037	1.91
Hubei	2,546,454	6,125,416	2.41	348,608	822,122	2.36
Hunan	1,274,100	2,655,163	2.08	536,084	972,148	1.81
Guangdong	9,094,900	28,537,400	3.14	20,842,500	49,876,300	2.39
Guangxi	2,519,770	5181226	2.06	1,003,160	2,008,882	2.00
Hainan	469,787	1,158,532	2.47	131,984	238,752	1.81
Chongqing	1,189,992	6,306,958	5.30	192,882	1,022,275	5.30
Sichuan	2,192,328	4,126,475	1.88	410,291	744,708	1.82
Guizhou	318,574	605,461	1.90	150,245	263,777	1.76
Yunnan	4,506,937	8,316,547	1.85	659,978	1,310,968	1.99
Tibet	211,172	635,564	3.01	38,867	122,361	3.15
Shaanxi	2,285,189	9,769,322	4.28	395,839	1,154,735	2.92
Gansu	39,624	61,956	1.56	9463	12,799	1.35
Qinghai	50,349	176,222	3.50	8083	28,291	3.50
Ningxia	23,521	91,732	3.90	4052	15,803	3.90
Xinjiang	515,585	2,013,859	3.91	16,832	69,100	4.11
Locality	Macau compatriots			Taiwan compatriots		
Total	4,937,650	11,660,502	3.53	13,853,595	42,342,375	3.51
Beijing	16,264	69,935	4.30	248,507	1,068,580	4.30
Tianjin	3220	77,685	24.13	49,594	1,139,719	22.98
Hebei	42,735	91,433	2.14	66,504	155,549	2.34
Shanxi	36,913	108,191	2.93	91,981	252,048	2.74

(continued)

Table B.7 (continued)

Locality	Foreigners			Hongkong compatriots		
	Arrivals	Nights	Average stay	Arrivals	Nights	Average stay
Inner Mongolia	19,633	97,560	4.97	35,288	162,652	4.61
Liaoning	73,599	164,326	2.23	275,748	764,916	2.77
Jilin	15275	35,902	2.35	86,088	211,058	2.45
Heilongjiang	555	2077	3.74	37,815	65,346	1.73
Shanghai	19,364	77,710	4.01	682,148	2,601,761	3.81
Jiangsu	8219	19,760	2.40	955,808	4,411,257	4.62
Zhejiang	122,075	383,609	3.14	791,102	1,696,563	2.14
Anhui	184,884	548,236	2.97	698,225	1,601,413	2.29
Fujian	153,902	690,828	4.49	2,082,925	8,753,433	4.20
Jiangxi	308,208	577,015	1.87	299,783	580,682	1.94
Shandong	102,746	270,432	2.63	402,438	1,263,336	3.14
Henan	95,446	199,415	2.09	239,428	449,801	1.88
Hubei	42,189	84,712	2.01	438,377	994,219	2.27
Hunan	231997	400,842	1.73	365,874	682,913	1.87
Guangdong	2,483,900	5,610,800	2.26	2,650,800	6,680,600	2.52
Guangxi	309,706	626,242	2.02	992,524	2,140,602	2.16
Hainan	11,098	20,436	1.84	136,000	228,174	1.68
Chongqing	27,618	146,375	5.30	398,370	2,111,361	5.30
Sichuan	74,532	122,106	1.64	410,767	671,584	1.63
Guizhou	70,533	110,007	1.56	183,531	355,783	1.94
Yunnan	207,756	452,972	2.18	629,081	1,635,365	2.60
Tibet	22,652	74,937	3.31	49,211	160,802	3.27
Shaanxi	242,789	564,429	2.32	458,230	1,161,818	2.54
Gansu	2103	3223	1.53	20,289	28,277	1.39
Qinghai	4082	15,199	3.72	7568	28,002	3.70
Ningxia	565	2204	3.90	23,039	89,852	3.90
Xinjiang	3092	11,904	3.85	46,552	194,909	4.19

Source The Yearbook of China's Tourism Statistics 2017

Table B.8 International tourist arrivals according to locality 2016 (Unit: 10,000 Peoples)

Locality	Total (Ten thousand)	Japan	Ro korea	Malaysia	Philippines	Singapore	Thailand
Total	33,211,108	5,816,934	9,014,882	2,598,448	763,524	2,244,186	212,792
Beijing	3,547,619	248,261	379,410	80,773	20,892	119,199	53,686
Tianjin	718,904	217,215	170,432	12,183	2960	20,018	2266
Hebei	659,877	71,360	76,024	34,148	13,680	29,940	18,392
Shanxi	404,221	18,532	123,298	15,937	1104	17,033	6691
Inner mongolia	1,682,734	27,382	22,771	6097	1091	6590	3164
Liaoning	2,122,140	542,122	874,746	23,179	12,408	38,646	8992
Jilin	1,421,729	55,445	853,083	4181	4191	49,670	4180
Heilongjiang	908,707	22,918	111,199	3960	451	3090	1517
Shanghai	5,725,655	791,411	750,157	158,553	310,218	167,014	79,038
Jiangsu	2,179,954	414,889	407,723	91,107	28,284	68,466	25,793
Zhejiang	3,873,006	268,800	814,679	134,157	31,029	85,499	52,698
Anhui	1,844,596	119,013	633,825	77,849	11,437	89,977	38,182
Fujian	2,541,193	343,113	184,186	374,113	97,548	248,712	36,338
Jiangxi	498,020	32,655	58,627	17,493	8129	21,585	20,323
Shandong	2,376,575	289,620	163,485	42,736	33,994	70,015	16,147
Henan	958,064	67,445	344,367	35,052	8832	29,947	24,220
Hubei	2,546,454	510,972	165,065	80,635	10,800	92,374	23,304
Hunan	1,274,100	66,575	519,845	88,521	9844	32,804	54,058
Guangdong	9,094,900	1,015,426	577,584	395,384	67,626	313,165	185,529
Guangxi	2,519,770	59,578	403,583	287,182	39,395	154,324	96,006
Hainan	469,787	9934	64,489	49,754	2574	37,080	13,635
Chongqing	1,189,992	113,223	340,754	56,317	7070	60,562	97,695
Sichuan	2,192,328	202,858	175,993	146,532	16,610	139,719	78,115

(continued)

Table B.8 (continued)

Locality	Total (Ten thousand)	Japan	Ro korea	Malaysia	Philippines	Singapore	Thailand
Guizhou	318,574	23,074	35,163	12,602	2019	12,954	6383
Yunnan	4,506,937	136,139	332,885	241,962	13,075	265,736	524,018
Tibet	211,172	9638	9298	11,541	1896	8968	4075
Shaanxi	2,285,189	115,270	401,291	103,793	5691	51,783	37,824
Gansu	39,624	8335	3913	4177	222	2741	1854
Qinghai	50,349	4910	5554	1697	0	1479	3037
Ningxia	23,521	2112	1650	1063	187	1461	513
Xinjiang	515,585	8709	9803	5770	267	3635	406
Locality	U.S.A.	Canada	U.K.	France	Germany	Russia	Australia
Total	1,308,535	1,513,753	1,901,984	1,611,100	1,959,020	2,850,847	1,415,093
Beijing	703,381	152,901	183,287	131,740	205,575	94,878	146,019
Tianjin	58,089	9518	16,476	12,190	24,056	2939	16,350
Hebei	25,908	13,813	28,131	23,947	26,051	49,135	13,823
Shanxi	28,294	8437	9274	935	11,961	6049	12,325
Inner Mongolia	14,425	5259	6132	7305	4947	600,102	4049
Liaoning	66,173	21,666	25,109	18,791	52,871	221,832	20,715
Jilin	18,104	11,505	11,437	12,811	61,593	287,979	14,040
Heilongjiang	5514	1638	1414	1597	2054	741,779	2120
Shanghai	696,127	167,809	187,279	167,266	242,847	91,718	170,104
Jiangsu	225,373	78,812	59,919	46,447	103,154	21,253	30,124
Zhejiang	368,802	84,860	103,325	80,576	146,442	46,315	78,674
Anhui	162,159	45,705	59,830	59,837	61,902	33,363	37,210
Fujian	303,981	68,770	70,189	44,309	67,181	27,541	77,493
Jiangxi	42,835	20,643	30,086	25,679	21,320	15,337	15,965

(continued)

Table B.8 (continued)

Locality	Total (Ten thousand)	Japan	Ro korea	Malaysia	Philippines	Singapore	Thailand
Shandong	153,285	38,780	63,215	48,373	66,679	70,262	43,028
Henan	56,969	50,818	34,886	35,021	35,772	35,438	16,072
Hubei	430,293	143,440	176,465	222,484	154,843	22,132	103,393
Hunan	74,906	30,801	43,140	33,252	30,095	35,025	25,614
Guangdong	754,468	167,033	164,223	152,930	156,765	102,985	165,342
Guangxi	134,230	63,026	69,710	67,551	53,482	15,923	51,748
Hainan	29,112	10,305	6707	6461	10,024	81,361	7804
Chongqing	116,730	32,501	33,797	28,733	44,326	13,149	30,233
Sichuan	336,390	82,926	204,582	87,345	112,230	19,691	102,907
Guizhou	33,542	12,504	17,988	21,493	11,313	11,439	9705
Yunnan	221,961	75,688	130,496	148,394	120,313	32,412	89,936
Tibet	23,981	9317	10,807	8345	10,691	9552	8213
Shaanxi	352,475	94,364	143,895	101,837	104,782	25,319	115,114
Gansu	3429	916	1231	1957	1536	492	1221
Qinghai	5232	1646	1669	1442	1580	914	1244
Ningxia	3227	702	597	517	1212	304	714
Xinjiang	8330	7650	6688	11,535	11,423	134,229	3794

Source The Yearbook of China's Tourism Statistics 2017

Table B.9 Number of star-rated hotels according to locality 2016 (Unit: 10,000 Peoples)

Locality	Star hotels	Five-star	Four-star	Three-star	Two-star	One-star
Total	9861	800	2363	4856	1771	71
Beijing	723	107	145	403	66	2
Tianjin	651	78	164	283	121	5
Hebei	622	30	146	378	68	0
Shanxi	561	85	156	251	69	0
Inner mongolia	559	17	71	210	239	22
Liaoning	419	18	64	222	113	2
Jilin	416	59	118	161	77	1
Heilongjiang	411	17	84	242	65	3
Shanghai	410	11	83	231	85	0
Jiangsu	364	19	78	171	91	5
Zhejiang	350	20	124	159	45	2
Anhui	349	25	72	186	64	2
Fujian	334	47	122	149	15	1
Jiangxi	312	23	106	142	40	1
Shandong	310	12	51	198	49	0
Henan	229	3	66	155	72	3
Hubei	298	21	80	127	68	2
Hunan	290	14	93	162	21	0
Guangdong	275	14	41	170	50	0
Guangxi	266	6	56	115	76	13
Hainan	227	67	66	67	26	1
Chongqing	198	6	46	109	36	1
Sichuan	197	28	48	94	27	0
Guizhou	194	16	52	100	26	0
Yunnan	175	10	28	78	59	0
Tibet	169	3	42	87	37	0
Shaanxi	124	25	39	52	5	3
Gansu	90	0	35	49	6	0
Qinghai	84	15	35	28	6	0
Ningxia	76	2	19	31	24	0
Xinjiang	108	2	33	46	25	2

Source The Yearbook of China's Tourism Statistics 2017

Table B.10 Daily expenditure of international overnight arrivals according to age and sex 2016 (Unit: US $/Night)

	(Average Expenditure) (US $/Night)	Foreigners	Hong Kong compatriots	Macao compatriots	Taiwan compatriots
General average	219.84	243.57	162.90	135.83	219.94
14 or under	255.45	321.48	148.39	87.52	134.28
15–24	197.89	217.61	154.72	125.80	210.06
25–44	217.54	245.08	152.91	134.36	217.56
45–64	234.34	252.41	192.13	150.41	227.87
65 or over	213.98	239.73	145.96	128.57	214.18
Male	218.84	241.59	166.21	136.46	210.76
Female	221.07	246.07	158.96	135.14	231.35
Official	247.87	253.84	243.74	202.16	224.45
Professional	205.65	237.11	143.79	131.14	195.25
Clerk	231.91	261.60	166.64	150.87	241.55
Technician/worker	200.38	215.26	138.54	142.58	226.98
Businessman	225.66	235.05	198.24	155.24	226.26
Waiter/salesmen	215.84	249.60	140.34	139.04	243.74
Retiree	218.96	265.72	141.87	128.26	196.51
Housewives	230.29	254.97	149.14	137.44	259.65
Servicemen	196.35	229.73	111.03	86.83	246.11
Students	192.39	216.83	153.69	91.18	174.06
Others	239.94	251.50	218.04	146.28	217.57
Sightseeing	242.49	253.27	226.13	162.48	238.56
Leisure/holiday	218.08	252.68	151.25	127.69	209.53
Visiting friends and relatives	155.36	189.19	120.29	94.72	197.37
Business	223.90	237.60	171.33	146.99	212.17
Meeting	259.62	297.24	185.05	154.36	253.51
Religion/pilgrimage	213.94	258.74	117.98	134.48	259.06
Cultural/sports/sci-tech exchange	185.25	220.06	134.39	81.87	137.90
Shopping	224.11	233.63	239.11	171.98	287.18
Health/medical care	227.99	273.49	147.43	198.24	69.15
Others	211.24	215.66	204.96	126.53	239.61

Source The 2016 sampling of expenditure by international visitors in China

Table B.11 Daily expenditure of international overnight arrivals by locality 2016

Locality	(Average Expenditure) (US $/Night)	Foreigners	Hong Kong compatriots	Macao compatriots	Taiwan compatriots
Beijing	264.42	265.52	250.03	272.62	253.22
Tianjin	219.35	220.89	211.76	210.54	217.46
Hebei	176.43	176.55	181.30	178.75	167.46
Shanxi	185.94	187.34	186.67	169.79	186.20
Inner Mongolia	200.76	202.41	178.72	205.05	195.27
Liaoning	212.63	214.95	197.96	202.37	193.06
Jilin	183.53	183.45	182.32	170.63	191.62
Heilongjiang	200.30	205.86	193.89	176.69	176.90
Shanghai	274.35	271.92	296.24	291.96	286.33
Jiangsu	239.96	241.34	236.08	231.04	238.24
Zhejiang	222.87	224.24	225.78	224.50	209.61
Anhui	195.99	195.67	193.33	196.73	203.03
Fujian	201.78	214.51	179.04	202.01	191.10
Jiangxi	170.95	176.68	158.94	157.92	168.39
Shandong	211.51	214.80	214.85	177.51	200.08
Henan	166.23	166.67	162.81	148.28	175.83
Hubei	198.95	210.11	172.16	183.73	195.79
Hunan	198.48	198.62	197.10	193.71	201.43
Guangdong	180.16	195.63	162.23	170.69	176.71
Guangxi	193.94	190.85	197.66	193.75	207.38
Hainan	189.59	189.82	184.50	194.38	192.83
Chongqing	196.16	198.61	172.43	174.16	197.55
Sichuan	193.32	192.96	192.35	194.31	196.34
Guizhou	189.29	192.27	177.12	177.63	185.91
Yunnan	206.76	210.21	189.34	187.11	198.83
Tibet	201.58	205.49	152.93	153.99	181.84
Shaanxi	195.17	195.01	199.21	200.72	217.09
Gansu	165.74	175.18	144.61	154.91	158.87
Qinghai	166.28	168.11	157.83	150.98	165.77
Ningxia	173.21	176.14	127.71	141.09	133.89
Xinjiang	180.51	180.60	179.90	175.00	183.26

Table B.12 Employees in China's tourism industry 2016 (Unit: Peoples)

Locality	Total	Star-rated hotel	Travel agency	Scenic spots
Total	2,830,489	1,196,564	346,219	1,287,706
Beijing	139,722	85,010	30,521	24,191
Tianjin	29,067	13,689	4593	10,785
Hebei	112,781	42,361	8575	61,845
Shanxi	49,434	24,498	8060	16,876
Inner Mongolia	39,839	17,283	6843	15,713
Liaoning	98,508	33,964	9444	55,100
Jilin	29,553	13,881	4688	10,984
Heilongjiang	49,727	12,996	5151	31,580
Shanghai	96,530	53,009	31,691	11,830
Jiangsu	181,744	79,965	34,809	66,970
Zhejiang	152,334	95,109	7889	49,336
Anhui	81,320	34,464	9781	37,075
Fujian	97,553	53,536	18,308	25,709
Jiangxi	97,376	26,332	6196	64,848
Shandong	247,490	79,378	21,049	147,063
Henan	104,451	45,662	6483	52,306
Hubei	94,070	34,569	16,638	42,863
Hunan	219,076	46,179	13,030	159,867
Guangdong	236,918	122,867	41,006	73,045
Guangxi	70,468	32,596	7898	29,974
Hainan	43,629	20,954	4525	18,150
Chongqing	57,766	28,506	6759	22,501
Sichuan	113,123	37,849	6456	68,818
Guizhou	47,175	18,654	2743	25,778
Yunnan	108,126	43,377	8464	56,285
Tibet	9333	3869	2380	3084
Shaanxi	90,900	34,504	9601	46,795
Gansu	46,098	22,125	4518	19,455
Qinghai	15,987	5798	2071	8118
Ningxia	12,841	6982	1618	4241
Xinjiang	57,550	26,598	4431	26,521

Source The Yearbook of China's Tourism Statistics 2017

Table B.13 Monthly international tourist arrivals according to purpose 2016 (Unit: 10,000 Peoples)

Month	Total	Meeting/business	Sightseeing/leisure	Visiting friends and relatives	Worker and crew	Others
Whole year	3148.38	579.74	1051.16	96.19	471.75	949.55
Jan.	208.76	42.44	55.52	7.10	30.46	73.23
Feb.	169.73	28.27	43.49	7.27	27.45	63.27
Mar.	243.77	50.50	79.79	8.02	33.97	71.49
Apr.	252.57	54.29	86.14	7.51	34.52	70.10
May	239.41	48.76	80.08	7.15	35.95	67.49
June	232.92	47.62	74.74	8.60	37.53	64.44
July	238.37	47.43	76.10	10.56	39.46	64.82
Aug.	239.47	44.93	70.00	8.09	38.65	77.80
Sept.	269.41	47.84	94.07	7.96	40.90	78.64
Oct.	374.89	62.90	143.19	7.67	51.38	109.74
Nov.	342.75	57.46	125.14	6.83	50.08	103.23
Dec.	336.33	47.31	122.89	9.44	51.40	105.29

Source The Yearbook of China's Tourism Statistics 2017

Table B.14 Developmental stage of international tourism receipts

Year	Tourism revenue(US $ Million)	Year cost
1994	≥ 5000	16
1996	$\geq 10{,}000$	2
2000	$\geq 1{,}500{,}000$	4
2002	$\geq 20{,}000$	2
2004	$\geq 25{,}000$	2
2006	$\geq 30{,}000$	2
2007	$\geq 40{,}000$	1
2011	≥ 2500	4
2016	≥ 5500	5

Source Based on the statistical data released by the National Tourism Administration over the years

Index

© Social Sciences Academic Press and Springer Nature Singapore Pte Ltd. 2019

P. Zhou, *The Theory and Practice of China's Tourism Economy (1978—2017)*, Research Series on the Chinese Dream and China's Development Path, https://doi.org/10.1007/978-981-32-9107-2

Printed by Printforce, the Netherlands